PROMISES TO KEEP

To my beautiful wife Gerardine

Promises to Keep

*A Woman's Medical Nightmare
and Her Husband's Search for the Truth*

JOHN GLEESON

SITRIC BOOKS

First published 2000 by
SITRIC BOOKS LTD
62–63 Sitric Road, Arbour Hill,
Dublin 7, Ireland

A CIP record for this title is available from
The British Library.

3 5 7 9 10 8 6 4 2

ISBN 1 903305 02 0

Set in Palatino
Printed in Ireland by Techman Ireland Ltd

Contents

... I have promises to keep,
And miles to go before I sleep,
And miles to go before I sleep.

(Robert Frost, 'Stopping by Woods on a Snowy Evening', 1923)

ONE / *Meeting Gerardine*

How nervous I used to be. She worked in O'Neill's newsagents after school and on Saturdays. She'd blush when I'd come in. There was that teenage awkwardness of not knowing where to look and I would try to be cool. I would browse through the magazines pretending to be looking for some particular one. I'd wait until other customers had left before I would make my move. 'Is *Mad* in yet?' I'd ask. She would blush even more and say, 'No, next week.' I'd say, 'Okay, thanks.' And that would be that. I'd stand on the pavement outside, hoping she was looking, and light up a cigarette, sheltering the flame from the non-existent wind like the hero did in all the best movies. I was seventeen years old and my heart was pounding.

Her best friend had told my best friend that she liked me. I thought she was gorgeous. She had shoulder-length auburn hair, a heart-shaped face, gorgeous green eyes. Her name was Gerardine Kelly. It could be because I loved her so much that I find even her name special, but I've always believed that a person's name plays a major part in who they are.

It was the evening of the 26th of August 1976 when the fairy tale began. I was walking into town to meet my friends. Outside a sweet-shop there was a small group of girls. I could hear them chatting. As I got closer, they became completely silent. I remember that I felt strangely self-conscious as I was passing them. 'Hello, Johnny,' they chorused, almost in unison. As I turned to reply, I noticed one girl standing at the back of the bunch with her head down, looking mortified.

'Hello, girls,' I said. They all had huge grins on their faces. I kept walking and when I'd gone about ten yards, I turned and looked back. At that moment she looked up and I realized who she was and why her friends had been giving her a hard time. Then it happened. I couldn't take my eyes off her and she wouldn't take her eyes off me. If someone had

12

dropped a piano on me, I don't think it would have affected me as much. It was the first time I had ever really looked at her and she was so beautiful. She smiled at me and then as the sound of her friends making fun of her began to invade our moment, she returned to looking at her feet.

As I continued on my way I felt a strange sense of contentment. I can't for the life of me remember any of the events of that day either before or after this encounter, but in the years that followed we often talked about that summer evening and our story-book beginning.

About a week later I met Gerardine again as I was coming home from the library. She used the excuse of asking me what book I was carrying. I told her, and our first real conversation began. The friends who had been with her picked up on the connection between us and drifted off. We talked and talked and it soon became clear that Gerardine knew a lot about me. She almost revelled in the knowledge of who I was and what I did. She knew the names of all the girls that I had gone out with. She knew where I lived. She knew how old I was. When she said she knew I played guitar I asked her if she would like to hear me play. As luck would have it, my house wasn't far away, so I collected the guitar.

At the top of a hill near where I lived was a bench overlooking the town. Like all benches it bore the scars of many declarations of love. We talked about everything we could think of. There was never an awkward moment. We smoked loads of fags, as was the style of our generation: it was cool to smoke in the '70s. When Gerardine asked me to play something for her I began to do my John Denver thing – his songs were very popular among budding guitarists at that time. Almost all of them were love songs, and, most importantly, they were easy to play. Without any embarrassment whatsoever, I serenaded that beautiful girl. When I had finished my party pieces and the scene was set, I kissed her.

The days and weeks that followed passed very quickly. We spent the last few days of the summer together. Then I would meet Gerardine after school and we would usually walk down to the river where we would sit together in the afternoon sun. There would be a lot of hand-holding and kissing and we would stay together until teatime. In the evenings I would meet her at the fountain and more hand-holding and kissing would follow. We would walk around the town and out the country roads. We would walk for miles talking about anything and everything that came into our heads. This was to be the pattern of our relationship from then on.

About this time I was beginning to make a bit of a name for myself as a guitar player, and together with some of my musical friends we formed a succession of bands. I remember we rehearsed for three weeks to play one gig in the local youth centre for a charity run by the St Vincent de Paul. The drummer's brother used to deliver milk for the Leix Dairy, and he borrowed the milk lorry and transported all our equipment for us. It must have been a comical sight with four of us sitting on the bed of this open-backed milk lorry, holding on to drums and amplifiers as he drove us through the town to our date with stardom.

I remember how proud Gerardine was of me as we set the night on fire with our versions of Jimi Hendrix's 'Hey Joe' and Eric Clapton's 'Layla'. To our peers we were the coolest men alive. Everybody cheered and screamed for more. The little shop ran out of Coke and fags. The car park and football pitch outside the gym where we were playing was awash with teenage passion, and all was right with the world. There would be many different bands and different gigs to come in the future for me, but that was the night when we became kings for an evening, and Gerardine was right there and part of it.

We would sometimes go to the local disco on weekends. Carlow was a small town, but that didn't make us naïve. We knew exactly what the real world was like. Gerardine had a grasp of life that was way beyond her years. She had a remarkable confidence in herself and as I got to know her it became obvious to me that I was completely in love with her. I have never lost that feeling. Even when we were in bad humour, there was never any doubt that we would always be together. She said that we should never let the sun go down on an argument.

Gerardine was the best and luckiest thing that has ever happened to me. I came from a large family that was devoid of any real love. I was one of ten children. There would have been a few more had they survived infancy. My mother spent most of her life struggling to make ends meet. My father had a good job and earned enough at the time to make life a lot easier than it was, but he spent a great deal of his wages on drink. The strain on my mother was very great. When I look back now I can appreciate the amazing job that she did just to bring us all up. My father never raised a hand to anyone, but his life was closed to all of us. In all the years that I knew him, I never had a conversation with him. He put food on the table and a roof over our heads and that was as far as he went. I think that drink was an escape for him. When he was full, he was happy and there would be no tension in the house. But when he was sober, he was sour and grumpy and you knew to stay away. When my mother would somehow save enough money to bring us to the seaside, my father would spend all his time in the pub. These holidays were happy times, though, and my mother loved them. She was always happy by the sea.

Meeting Gerardine was my beginning. She awakened a soft side in me that I had never been aware of. I suppose I needed someone to love me. I had grown up hard and I'm sure that if it hadn't been for her and the love that she gave me, I would have been a very different person altogether. We became inseparable to the almost complete exclusion of others. We still had our friends but as time progressed we spent more and more time together. The future was always the main topic of our discussions and we began to plan it. We would do everything right.

On the 22nd of June 1985 we were married in the Cathedral of the Assumption in Carlow. It was the best day of our lives. We had done everything by the book. We had good jobs, a new house, an almost new car and Rusty the Wonder Dog. For our honeymoon we went to Portugal. I remember an evening walk along the seashore. We sat down together on a low

wall. As we stared out at the bobbing lights of the fishing boats and the starlit sky, Gerardine turned her head to the side and looked at me. It was the same look that she had given me that day years earlier when she was being embarrassed by her friends. Now she said, 'I love you, Johnny.'

I smiled and told her that I loved her too. 'No,' she said firmly, 'you don't understand, I *love* you.' She had given herself completely to me. She was the most beautiful girl in the world and I was married to her.

'All we need now', she said, 'is a baby.'

TWO / *4 August 1993*

I was woken by the telephone. Its everyday sound had taken on a sharp note of urgency since Gerardine had been admitted to the National Maternity Hospital in Holles Street, Dublin, eight days previously. I rushed downstairs and managed to pick it up before the stilted message of the answering machine cut in.

'We think your wife will need an operation on her bowel, but don't be worried. If you would come up here as soon as you can – but take your time now, she's in no danger.' It was the voice of a nurse from Holles Street. She delivered the standard message well, and although the fear came I tried not to worry.

Now I was in a real muddle. Half of my mind was trying to grasp what she had said while the other half was trying to adjust to the general state of being awake. As I began falling back up the stairs, I tried to put some sort of order to what I had heard on the phone and fit it in to the already long-running saga of IVF, doctors, and the seemingly never-ending struggle that we were going through.

'Her bowel', the voice on the phone had said. *So that's what's wrong.* Through my fear, I felt a guarded relief that at last someone seemed to have discovered what the problem was. Despite the assurances during the past week that Gerardine was getting better and that everything was under control, to me her condition seemed to be getting steadily worse. I had made up my mind that today I was going to be firm with the hospital and insist that something definite should be done for her.

I had intended to do so on many occasions, but Gerardine was afraid that creating a fuss would antagonize them. All she wanted was to get better and go home. Gerardine was my wife and she was in pain. She had suffered so much and for so long that I tried not to add to her anxiety. Whenever I arrived at the hospital to find that she was almost crippled with pain, I bit my lip and trusted them.

*

ON A GOOD DAY, it takes an hour to get from Carlow to the outskirts of Dublin, and then another thirty minutes to get through the traffic to the hospital. I expected to get there at about 10.30. It was a Wednesday, the 4th of August 1993. For a change, traffic was light. The early-morning commuter circus was just about finished. It was a bright sunny morning with the promise of a beautiful day ahead. I had made the trip daily since Gerardine had been admitted, so I knew where I could park and where I had to go.

At 10.20 a.m. I was walking down the corridor of Unit 4 and into the gynaecological ward. Gerardine's bed was empty. The entire ward was empty except for one woman opposite. (It had been a bank holiday, and although it did not occur to us at the time, much of the staff had been on their holidays.) I assumed that Gerardine was being prepared for her operation. I still wasn't really worried. Yet from that moment as I stood by that empty bed to this moment, I have been living about as close to a nightmare as anyone can. By writing this story I hope that I can stand toe to toe with it, in some way learn to live with it. By reliving every moment, so that people can understand what

22

happened to my wife, I hope that I can achieve for myself at least some peace.

I walked back into the hall where the staff nurse's office was. Through the glass door I could see a nurse and a young doctor sitting by a desk. The nurse immediately rose when I opened the door. 'Here's Mr Gleeson now,' she said. I didn't recognize either of them. The young intern who had his back to me stopped writing and turned around. The nurse looked at me. Although her glance lasted no longer than a second, I have seen it over and over again in my mind ever since. Every part of my being knew that Gerardine was in serious trouble.

'Can you follow me, please?' The young doctor's voice sounded far away.

I followed both of them from the office and along the hallway. We stopped at a door painted in green gloss – hospital-green gloss. I could feel my legs beginning to tingle.

The door opened to reveal a black and white tiled floor, with brown gloss-painted walls. There were cardboard boxes stacked against one wall. In the centre of the floor they had placed a chair. This room had obviously been prepared in a hurry.

'Please sit down, Mr Gleeson.' The young doctor looked very ill at ease. He started to fidget. The last thing that he wanted to do was to break the bad news to me. He would have done this as part of his training, but it was perhaps more difficult for him than usual because he must have known that this should never have happened. As facts emerged in the weeks and months that followed, I often remembered how uncomfortable he had seemed.

'I'm afraid, Mr Gleeson, that your wife died at 10.15 this morning ...' There were more words but I didn't hear them. I heard the sound of my keys hitting the floor. I looked down and saw my hands shaking uncontrollably. I could feel my heart pounding in my ears. My lungs were heaving against my chest.

'That's impossible, that's stupid,' a voice screamed. 'She's just sick, that's all. Jesus Christ no, not Gerardine. It's that fucking IVF thing. No, no way. She can't be dead. You can't kill Gerardine, she can't die.' It was the strangest voice I had ever heard. It was filled with pleading, disbelief, desperate torment. I had never heard such a voice. It was my voice.

Strange thing, the human brain. Just when you think it's about to shut down, some chemical clicks in and suddenly you regain a kind of control.

The young doctor was speaking. Although I could hear him, his words had ceased to make sense. He was obviously having his own private nightmare.

'Where is she?' My voice was calm, my body still, my message clear. I was now like a robot. He continued to mumble. I couldn't understand a word.

Louder this time. 'Where the fuck is she?'

It worked. Although my voice was still calm, something in my words shocked him into action. Without another word he walked over to the door. The nurse followed him. I followed her.

Another green-gloss door. The doctor went in first, and the nurse held the door open for me to walk through, then she followed behind. This was a much bigger room than the last one. At the far end, they had created a corral of white screens – the type of screen you would normally see in wards, that provide a kind of mock privacy around beds. I followed the doctor, towards this ominous fragile box.

As I got closer, I could see shadows moving behind the screen. There was the sound of soft-soled shoes and hushed voices. The closer I got, the farther away it all seemed. I had to drag my legs across the few feet of floor by an act of pure will. I pulled back the edge of the nearest screen to reveal four or five shocked and alarmed people in white coats. The noise of my entry and the look on my face, coupled with their knowledge of what had happened, must have frightened the life out of them. As with the glance of the nurse minutes earlier, their expressions have burned themselves into my subconscious. Here they have found a home, and visit me from time to time. Sleeping has been something of a lottery.

Strangely, I can't remember the exact instant when I saw Gerardine, but at first it didn't look like they had the right woman. They all stepped back like children who had broken something. The bed had a half-naked woman lying in it. The woman was a strange colour. Her face didn't register with me as someone I knew. She had been left with one of her eyes half open. From her head to her chest she was a kind of a sickly yellow, but from her chest down to a white sheet over her hips she was a dark, bruised, almost black colour. On her chest were two distinct red marks – presumably the result of efforts to revive her. The black of her lower body, I discovered later, was caused by septicaemia or massive blood poisoning.

As I moved slowly towards the bed, I was trying to reconcile this ghastly form with anyone I knew. This certainly couldn't be my beautiful Gerardine. There was some terrible mistake. Why would they be showing me this poor unfortunate creature? As I got closer still, I started to recognize certain features and outlines that were strangely familiar. I was slowly beginning to realize that this tragic, wretched human being, lying now abandoned on this bed, was in fact my wife – once the most beautiful, the most loving of women. Here, lying in ruins, was all I had in the world. Here was the woman who possessed my heart and guarded it with her life. First denied the chance to give life, now denied the chance to live. That's when they started to run and hide.

THREE / *The Pillar Room*

Holding hands, we walked down the marbled corridors. The huge wooden frames on the walls told the names of benefactors and doctors, forever immortalized in gold writing. This was the Rotunda hospital in Dublin.

The surroundings were strange to us. They belonged to the mysterious world of medicine. It felt like some kind of enormous state within a state, with its own hierarchy and culture. Undeterred, we carried on to what was known as the Pillar Room. This was where Professor Robert Harrison was holding court, this was where we were going to find out about in vitro fertilization (IVF). The long road of trying to conceive a child had led us here. All the other methods had failed and now we were stepping into the unknown.

In the Pillar Room there were lines of chairs facing a long raised platform with a table and some chairs where the professor and his staff sat. As we found a place to sit we looked around at the other couples. There was an odd feeling in the room. Gathered here were people who had gone through the same disappointment as we had. We noticed that we looked about the youngest couple there. There was a sense that everyone was secretly observing everyone else. In some way it made us feel that at least we were not the only ones with a problem – I'm sure that was what most of the people there were thinking.

The professor started off the proceedings with stories of his successes with in vitro fertilization and how, with his help, a great number of us could have the child we longed for. He spoke at length of the procedure that they used to stimulate the woman's eggs: a series of injections and nasal sprays. He described how the regimen worked and went into a lot of technical detail about the theory and practice of IVF. He said that to his knowledge one woman had died from the procedure. I can see now that most of us were won over not by the man himself, but by the chance of conceiving, however tenuous.

When he finished we were given the opportunity to sign up. Couples who fitted the profile were likely to be accepted into the programme and start the necessary treatments as soon as the woman was at the appropriate stage of her menstrual cycle. Gerardine had done as much research as possible about the workings of IVF. She didn't like Professor Harrison's manner, but this was the only game in town. So we signed up and left thinking that finally we were in the hands of the experts, the people who knew how it worked.

WE STARTED the procedure in June 1991. Gerardine had blood tests at the Rotunda on Wednesday the 19th and Friday the 28th. On Tuesday the 16th of July we were interviewed by a social worker. (We discovered later when looking at Gerardine's file that the social worker had said we were very motivated and determined and thought we would be acceptable as candidates for the treatments. It is also worth mentioning that this was the one and only time that we received any support or counseling.) On Friday the 9th of August they tried what they called 'dummy transfer'. This would show whether, at the later stages of the treatment, it would be possible to place the fertilized eggs back into the uterus. This is one of the many normal hurdles encountered in the procedure; it went without a hitch and our confidence began to grow in a slow and guarded way. On the 12th of August I had to do a sperm test, the results of which we received on the 29th. Everything was fine; my sperm were bombing around and ready for action.

The treatment started on Friday the 20th of September when Gerardine's cycle began and they gave her her first scan. Then we went to the pharmacy in the hospital to collect all the drugs necessary for the coming month. We paid for them with a bank draft. On Friday the 27th Gerardine started the hormone injections; meanwhile, she went to Dublin periodically or scans. Around the 6th or 7th of October they decided that she would have to stop as the scans were showing what they thought were cysts on her ovaries. The danger here was that while stimulating the eggs, they would also be stimulating any cysts that might be on the ovary and there was a real possibility of developing ovarian hyperstimulation syndrome.

Ovarian hyperstimulation syndrome is the nightmare. It's the bogey man of IVF. Although with careful and regular monitoring the danger is reduced, it's always a very real and potentially devastating side effect of the drugs. Although we had been told that there was a certain danger involved, we had been won over by the positive sales pitch and by the possibility of conceiving. But now danger had reared its head.

So just before it was time to retrieve the eggs Gerardine was taken off the treatment. This was a huge disappointment for us. We had everything prepared. We had booked into a bed and breakfast in Drumcondra so that when the time came to have the eggs removed we would be close at hand. We had taken time off work and had put Rusty the Wonder Dog in kennels for a few days. We had told our friends that we were going away for a few days for a bit of a break. We had told the truth to nobody. If this thing worked and we had a child there was no way that we wanted anyone to know how the child had been conceived. We were very private people and this was our own very private business.

So off we went back home. Although we were disappointed that this form of the treatment had been stopped, we were told that we could try again: this time Gerardine would use a nasal spray. This is a different method of ovarian stimulation that is not as severe as the clomid (i.e. hormone) injections. Now we would have to wait until Gerardine's cycle started again. This arrived on October the 25th and, as instructed, she rang the hospital to begin the next phase.

In the meantime we had got back to our normal lives. We went to work and carried on as usual. When we talked about it we kept positive and always looked to the future, certain that the baby would come. Gerardine was a very determined woman, but she was also a very intelligent one. To say that she was obsessed with having a baby would be wrong. To say that she would have done anything, even sacrifice her own health, would be wrong. But Gerardine had an instinctive determination to become a mother. You hear of women going as far away as China to adopt a child. The procedures and obstacles involved in doing this are so incredibly difficult that you wonder why they do it. I marvel at the strength and resilience of the female sex. For I have seen with my own eyes my wife show the strength and courage of a thousand men. With Gerardine as with many other women, the desire to have a child is not an obsession, it's instinct.

ON NOVEMBER 14th 1991 we had an appointment at 11 o'clock where Gerardine would have a scan before starting the nasal spray. The woman's bladder has to be full for the scan. This distends the uterus so that it's possible to see what's going on inside. It also makes for a very uncomfortable journey. Even if your timing is perfect it means that for at least two hours before the scan you are not allowed to pee. Gerardine never complained as she sat cross-legged throughout the trip and in the waiting room, gritting her teeth, trying not to laugh at the humour in it or cry at the pain of it. She never faltered. Coming out when it was over she was like an Olympic champion heading for the loo for the longest and most deserved number one in history. Then it was back to the pharmacy for more drugs. This time it was a collection of nasal sprays and phials of clomid to be injected at certain times during the procedure.

On the 27th of November we went up to Dublin for another scan. They said that there was probably still a cyst on her right ovary, but that Gerardine should stay on the spray for three weeks and they would keep a close eye on it. On the 2nd of December we went up for another scan. They felt confident that the cyst wasn't growing any larger, so it was time to start the injections. For the next six days Gerardine went to our local GP with her little bag of drugs and he administered the injections. On Monday the 9th of December we went back up to the Rotunda for another scan. Everything seemed to be going according to plan. All the things that were supposed to be happening were happening. There would now be just one more injection of Profasi, another hormone drug, which she would have to have administered at 10.30 the next evening. If all went well they would try the egg removal two days later. Our hopes were understandably high, and although we tried not to tempt fate and talk too much about it, it was controlling our lives.

Gerardine would never let her guard down, she never took any of this for granted. She would say that she hoped it would work, but would not allow herself to consider it a sure thing. I knew that she was desperately hopeful but afraid that if she spoke it aloud and it failed then she would be crushed. She wanted to keep something in reserve just in case it didn't work so she could have the strength to go on.

Thursday morning, the 12th of December. We had hardly slept the night before. We rose at five to be there for eight o'clock. Gerardine had everything prepared. She was told not to eat a very big breakfast as this would be a medical procedure and she would be under anaesthetic. We left at about six o'clock and arrived at the Rotunda at about half seven. We went through the main building and out through the back into a small courtyard, to the IVF clinic that was tucked away in a small garden. We had come to know this place well over the past year or so, and today, we hoped, we would jump the biggest hurdle of all. If all went right today then the chances of conceiving our own baby would be very good indeed.

Gerardine was received by a nurse and taken away to be prepped. I was given a plastic container and told to supply my part of the equation. It seemed almost funny that as they led Gerardine into this room filled with screens, tubes and machines from floor to ceiling, my job seemed almost insignificant.

They recovered thirteen eggs from Gerardine's body, a very good haul indeed. Everyone seemed pleased, and we took great comfort that so far everything was going very well. All that needed to be done now was to put the eggs and sperm together in a controlled environment and let nature take over. All the hard work had been done. Gerardine felt very sick afterwards from the effects of the anaesthetic and had to lie down for quite a while until the feeling of nausea had passed.

We drove home trying not to read too much into what had occurred that day. Gerardine still felt a little sick and we had to stop a few times when she thought she was going to vomit. We arrived home at about five in the afternoon and she went straight to bed. I brought Rusty the Wonder Dog out for a walk. When Gerardine got up a couple of hours later we had our tea. She was feeling a bit better and the colour was beginning to return to her face. We went over the events of the day. It looked very good for us but she said that until she had a baby in her arms she was not going to start counting chickens just yet.

There was good news the next day. When we rang the hospital we were told that the eggs and sperm had fertilized. The staff were very positive now and told us to come back up to Dublin the next day for the relatively simple procedure of transferring the fertilized eggs back into the uterus. Gerardine had already done a dummy run for this procedure and had encountered no problems with it. We were walking on air. In twenty-four hours' time we could begin the new lottery of pregnancy. To get pregnant was one thing. To hold on to it for the nine months was something else. We looked to the latter now as our next battle. With all the skill of a field marshal Gerardine spent most of the evening formulating a plan for the next nine months.

When we arrived at the clinic the next morning we noticed right away that the staff were no longer smiling when they saw us. I remember wondering why we were being kept waiting. This is never a good sign. We sat in the hallway for quite a while, all the time clinging to our 'foregone conclusion' but becoming more worried as the time for the egg transfer came closer and eventually went by without a word from anyone.

Finally the doctor that we had been dealing with came out of a room at the end of the hall and asked us to follow her to another room. She motioned us to some chairs and sat on the edge of a table close by the window. 'I'm afraid I have some bad news,' she said. 'The eggs have all degenerated overnight and are all almost dead. Just why this happened I'm afraid we don't know. We have never seen this or heard of this before and we are all very disappointed that at this stage something like this has happened.'

I remember hearing Gerardine breathe out a long and tortured sigh. It was the only reaction that she gave. She turned towards me and gritted her teeth to hide her disappointment. What I witnessed made me feel small and insignificant. I knew the pain that she was going through. I knew the suffering, both physical and mental, that she had been through and I saw the unbelievable strength of this woman who would not let this devastating news break her.

The doctor said that they would like us to try again in three months' time. This time they would try a different medium to fertilize the eggs and they would hope that this would make the difference. Still in shock, we thanked her and walked out of the room and the building. We didn't speak as we walked to the car and started our journey home. As we left the city behind and approached Naas, Gerardine asked me to pull in. I stopped the car at the side of the road and she got out, leaving her door open. I followed from my side and as I approached her she waved me away. I stood frozen in my tracks. She looked across a low hedge with a vacant stare. Her body was rigid with emotion. All I could do was stand close by and watch the torment take hold of her. I didn't see the first tear, but it soon became a torrent and she began to shake. I sprang from the car to put my arms around her but again she pushed me away.

'If I don't cry I'll die,' she said through her tears, but her words were measured as though she knew that it was the time to let some of it out. She understood her own emotions better than anyone I have ever known, and this was all that was left for her to do to try and deal with what I knew was tearing at her very soul.

FOUR / *Belfast*

We tried IVF a second time in Dublin; again it failed. The staff at the Rotunda weren't able to explain to us why the treatment hadn't worked. All they could do was make a guess that there was something wrong with Gerardine's eggs that was preventing them from multiplying and causing them to die after fertilization.

Our last hope of having our own child now was to consider using donor eggs. In this process, eggs are donated by another woman and fertilized by the host mother's husband before being transferred into the uterus of the host mother. Because this procedure could not be carried out in the Republic of Ireland, we were referred by Professor Harrison's clinic to the

Royal Victoria Hospital in Belfast and Dr Anthony Ivor Traub.

We were told that there was a waiting list of over a year because the demand for donated eggs was so much greater than the supply. The only way we could move up the list was to find someone who already had children who would consent to donate her eggs. If this donor was a sibling, the harvested eggs would be given to a woman at the front of the queue and Gerardine would receive eggs from another, anonymous donor. This way, if a child were conceived there could be no family conflict about its parentage.

We needed help, and we found it. Gerardine's sister, Noelline, had two beautiful children, a girl and a boy. Although Gerardine was very close to her sisters and had indicated to them that we were ready to start a family, we had given no hint to them about what she had already been through. As far as they knew we were just taking our time. We now had to break our silence and tell the whole story to Noelline. It was a Saturday evening when Noelline arrived at our house for one of her usual chats with Gerardine. I remember that Gerardine asked me to wait in the living room.

Gerardine spared Noelline none of the details. She

told her all the facts, the apprehension that would be involved as well as the sheer discomfort. She told her too about our own sickening disappointments of the previous two years. Knowing exactly what would be involved, Noelline agreed without hesitation to donate her eggs. This act of pure selflessness I will remember until the day I die.

Early in 1992 we travelled to Belfast. This time there were three of us. We had an appointment with Dr Traub at his private clinic on the outskirts of the city. As before, Gerardine had everything prepared for our journey. The trips up to Dublin would pale into insignificance compared with this. Because hospitals do all their major work early in the mornings, our journeys to Belfast would have to begin very early. Undeterred as always, Gerardine set about the logistics of it all. It's about 150 miles from Carlow to Belfast, via Dublin. We would have to leave our house between 4 a.m. and 5 a.m. and collect Noelline on the way. Gerardine stowed all the provisions necessary for a long journey in a cardboard box on the back seat of the car, and off we went along the dark and deserted winter roads. It was the first time Gerardine and Noelline had ever visited Northern Ireland. There was no cease-fire at that time. I can't say we were in fear of being blown up, but like all 'southerners' who had never crossed the border before, we were apprehensive. My knowledge of Northern Ireland was limited to the stories of bombs, marches and soldiers we'd seen on the TV or read about in the papers – and the vague memories of rebel songs I'd learned years earlier courtesy of the Christian Brothers.

As we drove into the dawn we could see signs of life as the country began to wake up. We arrived at the border at about 7 a.m. The car became strangely quiet as we drove slowly over the ramps and up to the checkpoint where heavily armed and nervous young British soldiers were checking the traffic. I thought that with our southern numberplates we would surely be stopped and questioned about who we were, where we were going and what business we had in the North. A traffic light controlled the flow of cars and trucks through the checkpoint. We stopped at the red light. It wasn't quite daylight yet, but I could just make out the barrel of a heavy machine gun poking out of a long slit in a reinforced concrete bunker. I couldn't help but feel a little nervous sitting there while they checked out our numberplate on their computer. Eventually the light turned green, and we continued on our way. We were now officially in Northern Ireland. We drove through Newry and on towards Belfast. Apart from the road surfaces being much better than we were used to at home, the countryside and the houses looked just the same. Every now and then we would see a Union Jack flying on a flagpole in a front garden or on a public building. In some towns we noticed murals, and kerbstones painted in the colours of whatever flag that neighbourhood had allegiance to.

When we arrived at the outskirts of Belfast, Gerardine, much to the amazement of Noelline and myself, produced a map with a page attached giving all the instructions necessary to find our way to Dr Traub's consulting rooms. So with Gerardine as the co-pilot calling out instructions, we landed safely at our destination without a hitch. We were early, so we went and had tea in a café nearby. Right on time, we entered the clinic. The receptionist asked us to wait, and after about ten minutes we were ushered into the doctor's office. He asked Noelline to wait outside and gestured to us to sit. He spent some time silently reading notes that he had in a folder. We just sat there waiting for him to finish. It seemed to take forever. Eventually he asked us some questions about the IVF treatments used in the Rotunda. We explained to him what Gerardine had been through and the reason why they had referred us to him. We told him that they suspected that the eggs were the problem, but that they couldn't be sure because they had never seen a failure at that particular stage before. We explained that the woman with us was Gerardine's sister, a mother of two, who was willing to donate her eggs.

Dr Traub said that he would take Gerardine on as a patient, but his next sentence surprised us. He recommended that Gerardine undergo IVF again, using her own eggs, in the Royal Victoria Hospital. We pointed out that it had already failed twice in Dublin. He said that his treatment was different and he felt optimistic that it would succeed. He then asked us to visit the infertility clinic at the Royal Victoria for blood tests to see if we were free from hepatitis, HIV and other viruses. If these tests were negative, then we could start the treatment around December. We thanked him and left. Outside, we explained to Noelline what he had said. She was hopeful that this time it would work out for us, but assured us that she would still be willing to donate her eggs if this didn't work.

Gerardine started her third IVF treatment on 9 December 1992. The following day, we went back to the Royal Vic to go through the treatment with the nursing staff and sign consent forms. The formalities were over quickly and the rest of the day was ours. Gerardine liked to shop, and at the time shops such as Boots, Argus and Debenhams had no branches in the south. Things were cheaper in Belfast too, so Gerardine, always good with money, managed to combine an IVF-treatment trip with a little cut-price, pre-Christmas shopping. The fact that we were now paying for our third IVF treatment without a loan from anyone was testimony to Gerardine's ability to make a little money go a long way. She was never mean, but always knew where the best bargains were. We bought a vacuum cleaner, had something to eat and then made our way home.

On Thursday 17 December we were back in Belfast for more blood tests. (By this stage we were passing through the border posts with all the indifference of seasoned travellers.) These tests were to determine what kind of serum they were going to use in the culture where the eggs and sperm would hopefully fertilize and grow. Gerardine continued on the nasal spray all over Christmas and we returned to Belfast on 3 January 1993. Our appointment was at 9.30 a.m. and Gerardine had a scan. They said that everything was fine and egg collection would take place the following Tuesday. Back over the border we went on the Tuesday morning. They recovered nine eggs. They were well pleased, but we knew enough by now to hold off on the celebrations. The biggest hurdle lay just days ahead.

The following day we rang the hospital to be told that the eggs had fertilized and all looked normal. Still, we resisted the urge to feel excited. We had been to this point twice before. They told us to telephone the next afternoon. By then, they should be able to tell whether the cells were starting to multiply or not. Gerardine rang at four o'clock and was told that there were two cells and everything still looked okay. We were beginning to dare to hope. With her heart pounding and her nerves frayed, she rang again at six o'clock. This time there were four cells and the nurse told us to come up to Belfast in the morning. Although there was still a chance that they might die off, the procedure now was to transfer the fertilized eggs as soon as they reached eight cells or so, and that would hopefully be sometime in the morning.

On Friday, January 8th, they transferred the fertilized eggs into Gerardine's uterus and she started taking the hormone injections that would make the womb receptive to its potential occupant. As we drove home, we talked of what had happened for the first time. With all the disappointments so far, we had stayed clear of discussing what might happen if the eggs didn't die. Gerardine sat very straight in the seat all the way home, almost afraid to move in case she would dislodge her precious cargo that she had suffered so much to attain. The following Monday, Gerardine went back to work. We carried on as though nothing had happened. Apart from Noelline, nobody at home knew what was happening. Within two weeks, we would know whether or not Gerardine was pregnant.

On Thursday, January 14th, Gerardine began to feel a pain in her left side. She was still receiving the hormone injections every second day and didn't pay too much attention to the pain at first. By Sunday, her legs felt very heavy and shaky. On Monday, she felt sick, had some back pain and was very irritable. On Tuesday, she had slight stomach cramps and still the back pain.

One of the greatest dangers in the IVF procedure at this stage is an ectopic pregnancy. This is when the fertilized egg gets stuck in the fallopian tubes and begins the pregnancy there. This would require immediate surgery to remove the pregnancy or the woman would die. On Wednesday, Gerardine still had the pain in her back and felt nauseated. She rang the hospital and told them about the pain. They told her that some discomfort was to be expected because of the procedure she had just been through and if she would relax and take it easy then everything should be all right. On Saturday, January 23rd, she woke up at 4 a.m. with a stabbing pain in her back. I was asleep and it wasn't until the next morning that she told me that she had slept on the cold bathroom floor to try to ease the pain. When I asked her about the pain now she said that it wasn't too bad and she thought that maybe it was finally going away.

On Monday, Gerardine bought a home pregnancy test. The little white window turned pink. The sight that makes so many teenage schoolgirls cry in despair made my beautiful wife beam from ear to ear. She was pregnant. She came down the stairs with a look of sheer joy. For the first time since we had started trying to have a child, Gerardine was allowing herself a moment to believe it was possible. She allowed her guard to drop just a little. 'Now', she said, 'the real worry starts. I'm going to do everything I can to hold on to this pregnancy.'

On Tuesday morning, Gerardine felt sick again when she woke up. She came home from work early and went to bed. The next day she asked me to ring her office to say that she would not be in. I rang and told them and then made her a cup of tea. She said that she was still getting the pain in her back and that she would ring our G.P. a little later. I was told to go to work, not to worry, and that she'd see me at lunchtime. I went to work, but I was worried sick. I knew that her fear was that the pregnancy might be in the fallopian tube. If that were the case, it would be a tragedy and would almost certainly put paid to our hopes of conceiving a baby through IVF.

At about 10 a.m., Gerardine rang me to tell me to come home. She had rung our G.P. and explained her pain to him. He told her that he would make arrangements straight away for her to be admitted to St Luke's hospital in Kilkenny. He told her not to wait another minute, but to ring me and to get there as fast as we could. When I got home, Gerardine was sitting in the kitchen with a packed bag at her feet. She looked very pale and was obviously in pain. I put her in the car as gently as I could and tore off like a madman towards Kilkenny. It took a little over twenty minutes to cover the twenty-four-odd miles to the hospital.

After some confusion at reception, Gerardine was brought up to the gynaecological ward. I went off to park the car and when I returned they had put her in a bed where she was waiting for the consultant to come and examine her. They told me that it would be better if I stayed outside so as not to get in the way. When she saw me she waved and then with her usual thoroughness began to explain to the nurse the circumstances that had led her here. Dr Moran, the consultant, arrived and carried out an ultrasound scan. He said that he was worried that because of the IVF, there might be an ectopic pregnancy. As he examined her with the ultrasound, he became quite worried and said that he didn't like what he was seeing and would have to take a closer look. Eventually he said that he would have make a small incision in the body to allow a probe to see just what was happening. What they saw during this procedure made them decide on immediate surgery. Someone produced some forms for me to sign. I was finding it hard to take everything in.

They brought Gerardine down to the operating theatre and a very kind nurse left me in Gerardine's room with a cup of tea. Left on my own, I started to think. I just couldn't understand why, after everything Gerardine had been through and when we least expected it, something terrible would happen. I now prayed like I had never prayed before. I asked God to protect my beautiful wife. I prayed for an end to this nightmare. I made the point that Gerardine would be the most deserving of mothers. I pointed out all that she had been through and that she had definitely suffered enough.

It must have been an hour later when the nurse came to fetch me. She brought me down to the operating theatre where Dr Moran was waiting to talk to me. We walked down the stairs and I saw him dressed in his surgical attire. 'Your wife is fine, Mr Gleeson,

but I'm afraid her condition was very serious indeed,'
he said. He produced two photographs. He explained
that because of the drugs Gerardine had been taking
to stimulate the ovaries and produce eggs, the ovaries
had become hyperstimulated. One of her ovaries had
become hugely distended and gangrenous. He had
had to remove this immediately before it burst and
poisoned her whole body. The other ovary was almost
as bad but he was able to save almost three quarters of
it. This would be very important later on, because
without functioning ovaries a woman becomes
menopausal and Gerardine was far too young to have
that heaped upon her as well. I could clearly see in the
photographs the damage that the hormone injections
had done to Gerardine's body. Dr Moran explained
that because of the fairly major surgery that she had
just gone through, there would be little chance that
the already tenuous pregnancy would survive in the
uterus. I thanked him from the bottom of my heart for
saving my wife's life. The nurse then led me away,
saying that they were now going to bring Gerardine
back up to her room and that when she was comfortable, I would be able to see her. I sat in the corridor
waiting and watching for her return. I wanted to

make sure that I would be there when she woke up. I knew that I would be the first person she would be looking for.

FIVE / *The Letter*

26 February 1993

Dear Mrs Gleeson

I was glad to get the opportunity to talk to you on the tele-phone and to hear that you are gradually recovering from your dreadful experience. I hope that I was able to encourage you to come back and see us either for IVF or for treatment with ovum donation. The decision as to which of these treatments you would prefer I would leave entirely up to you and your husband. Please do not hesitate to contact me at any time in the future if you have any questions or worries.

Yours sincerely
A I Traub MD FRCOG
Consultant Obstetrician & Gynaecologist

IT WAS NOW almost five years since we had decided to try to start a family. In that time we had used every method available to achieve conception. So now here we were. Gerardine had started out as a strong and completely healthy woman, with her hopes, dreams and body intact. Now she despaired. The time after the surgery was very difficult. We were still trying to come to terms with all that had happened. The one thing that we knew for sure was that she would never do IVF again. We had reconciled ourselves to a life without children. The chances of conceiving now were worse than ever. Apart from the original mysterious cause of infertility, now Gerardine had only three quarters of one ovary left. Her recovery was slow and painful. The damage to her body was extensive, with a long scar right across her stomach where the surgeon had entered to remove the gangrenous ovary.

I watched Gerardine pull herself back together. I watched as she found the strength to carry on with our lives. I witnessed the bravest person I have ever known stand up and face a world that would now be childless for her. There would be no more talk of happy families. In her heart of hearts Gerardine must have sobbed an ocean of tears.

Then the letter arrived. We didn't know how to react to it, but we hoped that it meant that we would be able to try to conceive using donor eggs, and that we wouldn't have to wait too long to try this procedure. We made an appointment to see Dr Traub on Friday the 30th of April 1993 at his rooms in Belfast. We arrived at half-nine and were shown into his office. He said how sorry he was that everything had gone so terribly wrong. We sat down and Gerardine asked him if his letter meant that we could go on the programme of egg donation. She said that she would not consider doing IVF again and that egg donation was what we had come to Belfast for in the first place. Dr Traub replied that if we decided to try egg donation then we would have to go on the waiting list just like everyone else. He said that we would have to wait for up to two years for a place in the programme even if Gerardine's sister was willing to participate. We thanked him for his time, and as we made ourselves ready to leave Dr Traub smiled at Gerardine and said that another programme of IVF should not be out of the question.

'I only have three quarters of one ovary left,' Gerardine said to him, almost in disbelief.

'I have treated women here successfully with less than that,' he said. He went on to say that because Gerardine had become pregnant before the hyper-stimulation occurred, there was a good chance that it would work again. He said that this time he would use different drugs to stimulate the ovary and there would be absolutely no chance of the ovary being damaged. We were amazed. We couldn't take in what he was telling us. He replied to all of our questions with confidence, saying that the chances of IVF work-ing this time were very good and we should consider trying it again. We said that we would have to think long and hard about having another try at something that had nearly killed Gerardine.

All the way home we tried to reconcile ourselves to what he had said. We could not understand why he had been so opposed to egg donation for us. Maybe we had expected too much. But if it was really possi-ble to harvest eggs safely from the one remaining ovary then we would have to talk about it. After long discussions and soul-searching Gerardine decided to give IVF one last chance. After all she had suffered she was still childless and the chances of conceiving unaided were practically zero.

We returned to Belfast on the 19th of July 1993 to begin the treatment. Gerardine received a scan at the Royal Victoria from a female doctor who seemed to know the history of what had happened, and while she was doing the scan took a quick, almost fearful look at the side of Gerardine's body where all the damage had been done. We returned home with our collection of drugs and our list of instructions. The first injection would be on Wednesday the 21st.

On the 23rd we went down to Curracloe in Wexford for a few days' break beside the sea. Noelline had a mobile home down there and invited us down to give us a chance to relax and get some sea air. The weather was lovely. We arrived there in the early afternoon and Gerardine decided to go for a swim. Knowing the temperature of the Irish Sea in summer and being a big girl's blouse, I said that I would watch and hold the towel. We brought Noelline's little girl down to the beach with us. We each held one of her hands as we made our way towards the ocean. I can remember thinking that we were like a family then, with this little girl holding on to our hands and skipping along chatting to us in the happy language of children and cartoon characters. Gerardine swam in the cold water smiling and making fun of us 'scaredy-cats' on the beach, where we were making sand castles. I know that this scene made her happy. Her dream was still alive and one day soon we might have a child of our own here and our lives would be complete.

I had to leave after tea as I had some work to do back in Carlow, but I would be back the following day and we would spend the next few days together. When I got back to our house in Carlow after working late that night there was a message on the answering machine from Noelline. She said the Gerardine had developed pains in her lower back and she had brought her in to Wexford General Hospital where she explained in great detail to the staff there everything that had happened previously and that Gerardine was now on the IVF treatment. She said that Gerardine was comfortable and that I was not to worry. Gerardine had stopped taking the IVF medication and was being scanned regularly. Noelline said that I should wait until tomorrow to visit the hospital, as Gerardine was sleeping comfortably and in no danger.

I didn't sleep much that night and as early as I thought respectable made my way down to Wexford.

I found the ward where Gerardine was and as I walked in I saw her sitting up in bed. She immediately smiled that smile of hers to let me know that she was OK. I bombarded her with questions about what had happened and where the pain was. She said that the pain had eased a little bit overnight and that now that she had stopped taking the IVF injections she felt sure that any danger to her ovary would pass.

Gerardine's sister was there and said that when she brought Gerardine in to the hospital she had tried to contact Dr Traub. After many phone calls she traced him to his home. She explained to him what had happened. He said that he couldn't understand what was wrong and promised to ring the hospital. We stayed about two hours there and left when Gerardine said that she was tired and wanted to sleep for a while. I kissed her and said that I would be back that evening. She said no, that I should come back tomorrow evening, as this would allow the doctors to do what they had to do and we would know more then. So I went back to Carlow that night and collected some personal belongings that she had asked me to bring back with me the next evening.

I returned the next evening at about seven to find

Gerardine again sitting up in bed. She smiled and we kissed. She said that the doctors were unsure whether the ovary was getting smaller. She said that she was still in pain and she found it hard to go to the toilet. She held my hand tightly and looked into my eyes. 'Never again,' she said. I stayed for about two hours and then left for home saying that I loved her and would see her tomorrow evening, when we should know a bit more about her condition.

SIX / *Holles Street*

The phone rang at home about eleven the next morning. It was a nurse from Wexford hospital to say that they could not be sure about Gerardine's condition and were sending her to the National Maternity Hospital in Holles Street, Dublin, for expert care. She said that she would be taken there by ambulance and would arrive there sometime in the early evening. I immediately tried to get in touch with Dr Traub and finally got him about an hour later. He again said that he didn't know what was wrong. He said that Gerardine's condition should have started to improve as soon as she stopped taking the medication. I told him that she was now being transferred to Holles Street and he said that he would ring there later on in the day.

I arrived at Holles Street that evening and asked at reception where Gerardine Gleeson was. The woman I spoke to had no record of Gerardine. I explained that she was being transferred from Wexford General Hospital, and the woman said that she had probably not arrived yet, so I waited. About an hour later an ambulance arrived and the woman said that it was from Wexford, so I went outside as they were opening the back of the ambulance. It was Gerardine and she was being put in a wheelchair. Although she was obviously in pain, she smiled when the first thing that she saw was me. As they wheeled her inside I walked beside her and held her hand. We reached a ward where a nurse appeared and took charge of Gerardine. I was told to wait in the reception area as Gerardine was being admitted; when she was settled I could come up to Unit 4 and see her. All this took quite some time but eventually I was told that I could see her.

Again, as I entered the ward Gerardine was sitting up in bed and again she smiled at me. I kissed her and asked for all the details of what exactly was going on. All that Gerardine knew for sure was that in Wexford they felt that they didn't know enough about IVF and that's why they had transferred her here. She did say that she thought it funny that she wasn't transferred to the Rotunda, as she had been there before for IVF treatment.

I noticed that the ward was almost empty. There were about twelve beds and only three or four were occupied. I stayed with Gerardine until about ten and then left for home saying that I loved her and would see her tomorrow evening.

The next evening I arrived at the hospital to find no change in Gerardine's condition. Her tummy now was becoming noticeably distended and she said that she was still having trouble going to the toilet. I asked her if the doctors had told her what the problem was and she said that they were not sure. She said that she had been told by one doctor that they were going to drain off the fluid in the ovary the next day and that that should alleviate her pain. The doctor had said that the distended ovary was pushing against her bowel and that was why she was having trouble going to the toilet. Although Gerardine was in obvious discomfort, we chatted for a while and she seemed to be content with what she had been told. I left for home about half-nine that night and said that I would be back again the following evening.

The next evening, Thursday the 29th of July, I arrived at the hospital at about six. Gerardine met me with her usual smile and was sitting on the edge of her bed. She said that she had been to the toilet but was only able to go a little. I asked her what progress there had been with her treatment and she said that earlier that day she had been seen by a different doctor who said that everything was going OK. He said that they had read Gerardine's scan that day and that they were still considering draining the fluid from the ovary, but they were unsure whether the ovary had increased in size. I noticed that Gerardine's tummy was even more distended, but decided not to say anything. Gerardine was in the care of one of the most famous hospitals in the country and we felt at that time that they were doing their jobs. Although I was concerned that there seemed to be no real end to all this, I was not going to worry Gerardine any more than I knew she already was.

The ward was again almost empty; it seemed to me that it was almost closed down. Those patients that arrived seemed to be there for examination and didn't stay very long. The fact that this was the week leading up to the August bank holiday weekend didn't strike me at that time. It was much later, when we started putting the events together, that the significance of this particular week became apparent.

Friday the 30th of July. Day 4. As I walked into the ward that evening I was horrified at what I saw. Gerardine was lying propped up on the bed with a plastic tube coming from her nose, disappearing beneath the bed covers and connected to a clear plastic bag attached to the side of the bed. When she saw me she tried to smile, but it was more of a grimace than anything else. As I got closer to the bed there was a dreadful smell. It was obviously coming from the plastic bag at the side of the bed. Gerardine could clearly see the worry on my face and spoke quickly to allay my growing fear. 'Its OK,' she said. They had told her that they would have to drain off the fluid that was in the ovary and this was why she now had to have the tube inserted in her nose. At that time Gerardine was also on a drip, which struck me as odd considering that she had been unable to go to the toilet for almost a week now, and had told them so.

Just as she was trying to calm me down she suddenly asked me to reach under the bed and give her a blue plastic bowl. When I gave it to her she immediately began to vomit a brown, foul-smelling liquid into it. I didn't know what to do and ran down to the nurse's station. There was no nurse there, but I saw one in the corridor and chased after her. When I told her that Gerardine was vomiting she didn't seem overly concerned and said that she would follow me back to the ward to empty the bowl. All my instincts were telling me that something was very wrong here. Everything I had seen so far made me feel that Gerardine was just parked here. It was as if no one had taken responsibility for her, almost as if she was in the way.

When I returned to Gerardine's bed she had finished vomiting and was holding the bowl away from herself, as the smell from it was terrible. I took the bowl from her and as the nurse came into the ward I asked her where I could dump it. The nurse pointed to a small room at the side of the ward where I could see a large white enamel sink. 'Bring it into the sluice,' she said. I poured the liquid down the sink, washed the bowl out and returned to Gerardine's bed. When I got there I heard Gerardine say to the nurse, 'I am getting better, nurse, aren't I?' To which the nurse replied 'Yes, of course you are, you will be home by Saturday.' The significance of the question was lost on the nurse. She didn't know my wife. For the first time I could see fear in Gerardine's eyes. The nurse was saying what she had said a thousand times before to a thousand patients. The nurse was wrong. Gerardine was vomiting up her own faeces.

About an hour after the vomiting Gerardine said that she felt a bit better and that I should go home. She said that she was very tired and wanted to sleep now. I kissed her and told her that I loved her and then left for home wondering what, if any, treatment she was receiving. I was in a very difficult position. I know now that Gerardine, aware of my temper, was afraid that I would antagonize the hospital staff. She was in a terribly vulnerable position. She had to trust the staff to give her the best care, and was afraid to tell me that she was really worried, knowing that I would tear the place down and those in it if I suspected that they were putting my wife's life in danger. I drove home worried almost out of my mind.

Saturday the 31st of July. Day 5. With my heart in my mouth I stepped into the ward. What was I going to see now? To my immense relief Gerardine was sitting up in bed. The tube was gone. The smile of greeting was almost back to normal. She said that she felt a little better today and the vomiting had seemed to relieve her pain a little bit. She said that she was a bit worried that she was still having trouble going to the toilet and had told a doctor that earlier in the day. She also remarked that this was the third doctor she had seen since she had been admitted to the hospital. We talked about her condition and Gerardine said that she had rung her mother that day and asked her to come up to visit her the next day. When I left that evening I felt a little less worried. The fact that Gerardine's mother was going to visit her made me feel a bit more confident that we would be able to find out what treatment Gerardine was receiving. Gerardine's mother was herself a nurse of some thirty years' experience. She had recently retired from nursing and now was spending some time back in her native Co. Clare. Because we had been so private about the IVF, Gerardine's mother had been completely unaware that she was even in hospital.

Sunday the 1st of August. Day 6. I arrived to find the plastic tube back in Gerardine's nose. She also had been given back the plastic bowl and was getting sick into it from time to time. Because she received a bit of relief from her pain when she vomited and the vomiting had stopped before, we were not unduly worried that it had returned. Gerardine's abdomen was now extremely distended. She joked that, ironically, she now looked like a woman eleven months pregnant. She said that the doctor had told her that they were now sure that she had a urinary infection. Even though she was in great pain and discomfort, the assurance that now they knew what was wrong made her feel confident that it would only be a matter of time until she was well again.

Gerardine's mother arrived in the mid-afternoon and immediately asked the staff nurse to come to the bedside, because she was very concerned about her daughter's condition. The staff nurse went on the defensive, saying that they were now very sure what was wrong and that Gerardine was going to get the best possible treatment to make her well again. Gerardine said that she was worried that she was still not able to go to the toilet, and on hearing this Gerardine's mother said to the staff nurse that she was fearful that Gerardine would become dehydrated.

The staff nurse seemed to take exception to this and said, 'No one gets dehydrated in this hospital.'

She obviously resented the presence of Gerardine's mother. This was her ward and she was in charge. She then excused herself, saying that she had other things to attend to, and left.

Gerardine's mother said that she had no experience or professional knowledge of IVF treatment, but was worried about Gerardine's condition. She also witnessed the faecal vomiting and, although concerned, assumed it was a symptom of the IVF treatment. The staff nurse had made it very clear that she did not want Gerardine's mother to interfere. We stayed most of that Sunday evening and I drove Gerardine's mother back to Carlow at about seven.

Monday the 2nd of August. Day 7. I arrived in the afternoon to find the nasal tube gone, but the bowl still there. Gerardine said that she felt a bit better. The vomiting was helping to relieve her discomfort. She was back on the drip. I can only assume that what Gerardine's mother had said about becoming dehydrated had in fact got through to them, because she had been off the drip for some days before that. Gerardine had been told that they were convinced now that she had a urinary infection and had begun to treat her with antibiotics. Although there was no improve-

73

ment in her condition there didn't seem to be any real deterioration either and she was in good spirits. She was sure now that they had her condition under control. She was willing herself better. I know now that she was trying to be positive. She was determined to do all that she could to make herself recover. She had recovered from all the earlier disasters of this nightmare and she was determined that she was going to get better now as well. I left that evening, kissed her and told her that I loved her.

Tuesday the 3rd of August. Day 8. As I arrived in the early evening I immediately noticed that the hospital was busier. It then occurred to me that they were all back to work after the holiday. There were many more people about and the ward was becoming busier. I found Gerardine still in bed looking the same as she had the night before. She smiled at me and said that there was no change and that must be a good thing. She said that they were still giving her antibiotics to treat the 'urinary infection'. She was breathless for a lot of the time and found talking difficult. She had to speak in almost a whisper at times. Her tummy was still very distended and she found it hard to get comfortable in the bed. She said that she had seen yet another doctor that morning and told him that she was still having trouble trying to go to the toilet. Once again she was assured that everything was under control and told to try not to worry. She said that she was tired and I said that I would go for a walk for about an hour while she rested. I returned about seven and stayed for about an hour. As I always did I kissed her, told her that I loved her and that I would see her the next evening. As always she told me that she loved me back, and she told me that I was to make sure I got a proper dinner for myself. Even though she was going through this terrible ordeal, her main thought was for my well-being.

As I left her bedside I was not to know that that was the last time that I would ever see my beautiful Gerardine alive. That was that last kiss I would ever receive from her. Those were the last words I would ever hear her speak. That was the last time I would ever feel her arms around me.

SOMETIME BETWEEN 4.30 and 5.30 the next morning Gerardine's untreated bowel obstruction burst. The poison from her bowel now began to flow through her lower body. The septicaemia poisoning was massive. When the staff realized that she was gravely ill, at 5.45, they decided to telephone the consultant responsible for that ward. He advised contacting a consultant surgeon at another hospital. The consultant surgeon was contacted at 6.30. He said that he would see Gerardine at 8.30 that morning. At 10.15 that morning Gerardine died. It took three heart attacks to kill her. They waited too long to telephone me. They denied me the chance to be with my beautiful Gerardine when she died. I know that although dying, she had asked the staff if I was on my way. They no doubt reassured her that I was, knowing that I wouldn't make it in time. I know that she was holding on for me. I arrived at twenty past ten, five minutes too late.

IN THE EIGHT DAYS that Gerardine was in the National Maternity Hospital, she was never seen by a consultant. I would learn this fact and many more as I fought against the system to find out how my wife died.

SEVEN / *The Wild Flower*

My brother drove me home from Holles Street. It all seemed like a dream. The city passed by in an unrecognizable blur. I stared out the window of the car with my thoughts in turmoil. I felt like a child, helpless in a world he can't understand. I was in shock and like anyone in shock my mind had almost completely closed down. When a terrible event happens and the reality is just too much to bear, we find a kind of compromise with our bodies. We step into a parallel reality that protects us from going completely insane. To try to describe the way I felt immediately after Gerardine's death is very hard to do, even now. There was just enough control to sustain life and basic bodily functions. I noticed that some of my senses had deserted me. When people spoke to me I couldn't hear what they were saying. I could only see things that I was looking at directly. I don't remember feeling hot or cold, but I did remember the smell of the hospital and I still do.

We arrived home and as I approached the door of our house I could see that some of our neighbours were standing in front of me on the pathway. They had that look of disbelief and shock that only tragedy can produce. They spoke but I didn't hear and just nodded while focusing on reaching the door and getting inside. This house. This was a place that we had created together. Gerardine's beautiful flowers were everywhere, inside and out, and I needed to be there. I knew that I would be safe there. I don't think that the house has ever felt empty to me.

I BURIED GERARDINE three days later in St Mary's cemetery in Carlow. The grave is at the edge of the cemetery beside a line of trees. On the opposite side of the trees is the house where I was born, which is still owned by my family.

It was a very big funeral. Everybody liked Gerardine and I suppose a lot of people liked me too. I don't remember much about those days and I suppose that is probably best. I know that I cried like a baby for most of that time. I can remember how good and kind people were. Even today I find flowers that have been left on her grave; sometimes they don't even have cards on them.

I remember that the hearse broke down during the procession from the church and the cemetery. We all stopped on the road and waited until another hearse was found. A friend of mine walked over to me and said, 'She just doesn't want to leave you.'

About a year after Gerardine's death, I was tending to the grave as usual, putting fresh flowers down and plucking up any weeds that were trying to gain a foothold between the white stones that lay like a blanket on top of the grave. There was one little shoot sticking out from the top of the grave just under the headstone. I don't know why I didn't pluck it out like the others. I think I said to myself that I would do it tomorrow. The next day it had grown a little bigger and I still left it alone. Over the next week or so I watched as this plant produced a beautiful little bloom. I asked a friend of mine who is a bit of a flower expert to come and have a look at it. He said that it was a wild flower and the seed had probably blown onto the grave from some of the other hundreds of flowers in the cemetery. This made perfect sense, except that of all these hundreds of graves in the cemetery this was the only wild flower that I could find.

SOME DAYS AFTER the funeral, I received a call from the junior doctor I had met on that terrible morning in Holles Street. He asked me if I would come to the hospital to meet the Master, Dr Peter Boylan. He also said something that, had I been of sound mind at the time, would have made me stop and think seriously about everything that had happened in the hospital. He said that I might consider bringing a solicitor with me. Somewhere at the back of my mind there was an alarm bell, but being in the state that I was in, I didn't realize the full importance of what he had said.

Gerardine had gone to see Catherine Craig, a solicitor with P.J. Byrne & Company in Carlow, just after Dr Traub had encouraged her to try one last attempt at IVF. She had wanted to know if there was any legal protection for her, and explained to Kate what had happened. Kate told her that the law concerning the medical profession was a minefield. She advised caution and said that she would be available in the future if things went wrong again.

With the junior doctor's comment in mind, I went to see Kate the day before I was due to visit the hospital. She welcomed me and gave me her condolences. Like everyone else in town, she had heard of Gerardine's death. She said that she had been expecting me. I told her what the junior doctor had said to me on the phone and asked her if she would accompany me to the meeting with Dr Boylan the next afternoon. What she said made perfect sense at the time. She said that I would have a better chance of finding out the truth from Dr Boylan if I went on my own. She said that members of the medical profession tend to be extremely cautious in what they say when they are being listened to by someone from the legal profession. She said that if there was no blame to attach to the hospital then her being there might only prevent Dr Boylan from telling me what exactly had happened. She also said that if I wasn't satisfied with his explanation then I should come back to her and she would take it from there.

My appointment with Dr Boylan was for two o'clock in the afternoon. I arrived at the hospital the next day at about ten minutes to two. The woman on reception knew exactly who I was and asked me to wait. At about five past two a girl arrived and asked me to follow her. She looked at me a few times and finally said, 'Do I know you?' I was a little taken aback at this. I told her that I didn't think so, but I had been to a lot of places with a lot of bands and this wasn't the first time that someone had asked me that. She asked me what I was doing there. I was more taken aback at this. 'Do you not know what's happened?', I asked her and her face dropped. 'No,' she said and led the way. There was no more conversation between us.

She led me down a corridor and into Dr Boylan's office. The office was in two parts. The outer part was where his secretary had her desk and to the left of that was a door to the inner sanctum. The secretary asked me to wait and I sat in a chair close to the wall facing her desk. Some minutes passed and the door to his office opened. Dr Boylan was a tall man, well over six feet. He asked me to come in and in I went. He shook my hand and introduced himself. He said that he was sorry to hear of my wife's death and offered his condolences. He said that he had been away on holidays at the time and had arrived back the day Gerardine died. He asked me to sit down and I did. He sat on one side of a table and I sat at the other. I thought he looked like a reasonable man so I took Kate Craig's advice and simply said, 'What happened?' He shifted in his seat and looked out the window. He said that it was just one of those things and made the point that there was nobody to blame. He said that what they were looking at on the scans of Gerardine's abdomen looked like a hyperstimulated ovary – i.e. not a strangled bowel. He said that it was an unfortunate and tragic thing that had happened, but again, there was nobody to blame.

He did not tell me that Gerardine had never been seen by a consultant. He did not tell me that they suspected that she had a bowel obstruction days before it finally ruptured and killed her. The meeting lasted for no more than ten or fifteen minutes and before I knew what was happening, I was standing on the street outside the hospital. I have to say that to my everlasting shame, I allowed myself to believe what he had told me. I returned home and went straight to the cemetery.

*

SOMETIME LATER I had to return to Dublin to get Gerardine's death certificate. I got this in a registry office just off Baggot Street. The office was part of a clinic, which was very busy with people being tested for HIV. I sat there and waited for the registrar, probably looking as miserable as all the other people there. The woman in charge arrived and filled in all the required details on the death cert. I left the clinic and walked the short distance to the canal and sat down on a bench. Gerardine was now officially dead. I was now officially a widower. I started to cry. We had spent many happy times here in Dublin some years before when Gerardine worked in the ESB, and now I hated the place.

Back in Carlow, after a visit to the cemetery, I called in to see Mrs Kelly, Gerardine's mother. She invited me into the kitchen where I also met Gerardine's sister Pauline. They had just returned from Holles Street and a meeting with Dr Boylan and the staff nurse. Mrs Kelly was very upset and agitated. She began by saying that some days before, she had requested a meeting with the Master of the hospital.

She had asked for the staff nurse and a consultant on call at the time of Gerardine's death to be there too. I was a little surprised at this, but I realized that it would be only natural for Mrs Kelly to want to know what had happened to her daughter. I sat down and listened to what she had to say. Mrs Kelly had been a nurse all her adult life and was now retired. Pauline was also a nurse, having qualified some years before.

The two proceeded to recount what had happened at this meeting, which was attended by the Master and the staff nurse but not by the consultant who had been on call when Gerardine was admitted to Holles Street. Mrs Kelly said that Dr Boylan described the circumstances surrounding Gerardine's death as 'A pilot flying through clouds, without the proper navigation assistance'. She told me that she had had to stop him in mid-sentence. She told him that the more 'waffle' he was coming out with, the angrier she was becoming. In the end he produced some charts to support his story and she pushed them back at him, saying that it was all rubbish. She said that they all knew how Gerardine had died and all of this 'evidence' was rubbish. She left the meeting leaving them in no doubt that this wasn't over. She told me that in her opinion they had killed Gerardine and that this was something I should now realize. She said that she had come across a lot of arrogance in some thirty years as a nurse, but the attitude of these people made her sick to her stomach.

The buck should have stopped with Boylan. He had been away from the hospital for most of the time that Gerardine was there, returning to duty on the morning of her death, but it seems only reasonable to me that in the subsequent days, as the Master of the hospital and a doctor himself, he would have been informed of all the circumstances surrounding her death. It's my firm belief that he was trying to talk his hospital out of the position it was in. To a doctor, the word 'negligence' is something in the dictionary between 'nasty' and 'never'. Mrs Kelly went to Holles Street looking for a straight answer, but instead received a non-answer.

When Mrs Kelly and Pauline had finished telling me what had happened and what they themselves suspected to be true, I excused myself and went for a walk. I walked back up to the cemetery and sat down at Gerardine's grave. From where I sat I could see the bench on the hill where I had serenaded her on the night we met all those years before. It began to rain.

Slowly I started putting the events of Gerardine's eight days in Holles Street together in my mind. I must have sat there for a long time because when I left to walk home I was soaked and it was dark.

AS THE DAYS and weeks passed, I became increasingly obsessed with Gerardine's death. I would spend hours sitting at her grave, sometimes making up to four or five visits a day. In the quiet tranquillity of that place I was able to find a kind of peace. That was a very sad and surreal time. I had all but shut myself away from everyone. From time to time people would come and visit me, but I didn't want to be near anyone. I would arrange and re-arrange the flowers on her grave. I would trim the grass around the grave. I would polish the small plaque with Gerardine's name on it that the undertakers had made for the grave, and when I had the headstone erected, I would clean and polish that. When they erected the headstone, they put the usual grey limestone frame around the grave. Inside the frame they put a blanket of small white stones. The headstone is of black marble with gold writing and is cut in the shape of a book. The part of the grey stone frame where I sit has become smooth and shiny from my visits. It took a long time for my mind to settle itself into rational thought. Sitting by Gerardine's grave I slowly began to feel that the hospital had in fact stood by and let Gerardine die. The more I thought about what had happened, the guiltier they appeared. The real turning point was when Mrs Kelly told me what had happened when she visited Dr Boylan.

I returned to Kate Craig's office and instigated legal proceedings against the National Maternity Hospital and also against two individuals; the latter proceedings were eventually dropped. I also decided to try and find out the truth myself and did everything I thought possible to find the truth. Without the truth I knew that I would never be able to bury Gerardine. Without the truth I knew that the anger would become destructive. This anger that was slowly becoming so much a part of me was in a strange way the only thing that kept me going. Although it took a heavy toll on me emotionally, it gave me a reason to live. The pursuit of justice is an uphill struggle, as I was soon to discover. If you decide to go up against the system then you will find yourself almost friendless. You will be treated like a leper. You will be considered almost an enemy of the state and no one in authority will help you. The medical profession is untouchable. They have hundreds of years of tradition, respect and power on their side. They have their own culture and code of practice, but above all they have an instinct to protect their own. To try to prove medical negligence in Ireland is a task that should never be undertaken lightly. The mistake they made was failing to realize that I had nothing left to lose. They could not hurt me any more than they already had, and so I had nothing to fear from them.

IN THE FIRST MONTHS of my legal proceedings, Kate sought all the medical records and nurses' notes from Holles Street. These were very slow in coming, and almost a year had passed before we finally received the autopsy report. Kate told me at the very beginning that this was going to take a long time and that the other side would not be doing us any favours.

Slowly the real horror of what had happened to Gerardine began to emerge. Gerardine had died from a bowel obstruction that had been left untreated for over a week. The obstruction was caused by adhesions to the bowel from the scar tissue created after the emergency surgery in Kilkenny to remove the gangrenous ovary. The hospital notes show that a bowel obstruction was suspected in the first days of Gerardine's stay in the National Maternity Hospital, but they did nothing about it. Instead, they treated Gerardine for suspected ovarian hyperstimulation syndrome. The treatment made her bowel obstruction worse and hastened her death.

The consultant who was on call for that ward never saw Gerardine in all the time she was there. They had just parked her in the ward and passed her case from one junior doctor to another. If we had had private health insurance Gerardine would have been seen by a consultant gynaecologist. Gerardine always said we should get private insurance, but because we had spent all our money on the IVF treatment, this had to wait.

The first breakthrough in our legal case came when the hospital notes were given to John Bonnar, professor of obstetrics and gynaecology at Trinity College Dublin. He was and is by all accounts one of the most respected professors of obstetrics in the country and his opinion would be of great value. I believe that when Professor Bonnar was first approached with the hospital records he was reluctant to comment because he would know the people involved. I can only suppose that what I subsequently heard about him is true: that he is an honest and honourable man who takes his profession very seriously. I don't think that my debt to him can ever be repaid.

Professor Bonnar read the hospital notes, and the subsequent report that he produced left us in no doubt that the hospital and the hospital staff had been negligent. 'In my opinion,' he wrote, 'Gerardine Gleeson's death was the result of her care being provided by a large number of junior doctors with no direct consultant involvement. As a consequence the diagnosis and treatment of bowel obstruction was delayed and appropriate care was not provided by the National Maternity Hospital.' Another crucial passage reads:

'I am surprised that she was in hospital for one week and there is no record of a Consultant Gynaecologist having see her in the hospital. I could find no record of a Consultant having been contacted by the non-consultant hospital doctors until a few hours before the patient's death. Given the evidence of bowel obstruction from the persistent vomiting including faecal vomiting, a Consultant Surgeon should have seen the patient at least by the third or fourth day after her admission. In my view the patient did not receive an appropriate standard of care largely due to her care being provided by a large number of inexperienced medical staff and lack of consultant involvement in her diagnosis and management.'

EIGHT / *The Bin-Bag*

Professor Bonnar's report confirmed what we had already suspected to be true. It hardened me. I thought it strange at the time that although I was consumed with an almost primeval anger, I was in perfect control of myself. I found myself reacting as if I was pacing myself for the long and arduous task ahead. Even when the hospital sent me a bill for Gerardine's 'care', I took it in my stride. I telephoned the hospital and asked to speak to Dr Boylan, but he was busy. I politely told his secretary that I wasn't going to pay this bill and that I considered it in very bad taste indeed. She muttered a kind of confused apology and assured me that she would take care of it.

Shortly after the bill episode the hospital returned Gerardine's belongings in a black bin-bag. The bag was ripped at the side and the few belongings that she had were spilling out. The clothes inside were filthy. What she had been wearing at her death had just been bundled into the bag, and was covered with the issue of her last terrible hours alive. It was as if they were putting out the rubbish for the bin-men to collect. I can only assume that the significance of this particular act was lost on them. The bag was handed to Gerardine's sister Noelline by a hospital porter. There was also a nurse present at the time. When the nurse saw the look of horror on Noelline's face when she was presented with this torn rubbish sack, she sheepishly asked, 'How is the husband?' Noelline grabbed the bag from the porter and glared at the woman. 'How do you think he is?' she said, and walked out the main hospital door, down the steps and up the street in a flood of tears. I'm glad I wasn't there. Noelline had volunteered to collect Gerardine's belongings; she knew that I couldn't go near that hospital at that time. I'm not sure how I would have reacted to the bin-bag. Looking back, I think that it might have pushed me over the edge.

Gerardine's family washed and ironed her clothes and returned them to me neatly folded in a cardboard box. They waited quite a while before they told me about the rubbish sack. They were profoundly offended by it. When Noelline told me the story, she was crying. Her voice was shaking with sorrow and despair. She had been very close to Gerardine and I know that she will never forgive the hospital. None of us will. Some months later they sent me another bill. I haven't paid that one either.

IN OCTOBER of 1993 I began writing to the Department of Health in the hope that the minister, Brendan Howlin, would step in and bring the hospital to book. I was naïve enough to believe that he would make them tell the truth and change the system. Every time I wrote to his department I got the same reply, that the matter was receiving attention.

Eventually, in February of 1994, I decided to ambush the minister himself at one of his clinics in his constituency of Wexford. I arrived nice and early to make sure that I was at the top of the queue. I introduced myself to him and stated my business. I told him that the replies from his department were a waste of time and I asked him to do something before more women died unnecessarily. He was diplomatic enough and he promised to look in to it personally and get back to me as soon as possible. I thanked him and left him to his voters.

I had seen Mary Robinson's name on the heading of the hospital notepaper, so I decided to write to her too. Her secretary conveyed the president's condolences but stated that she was not involved in the day-to-day running of the hospital and was referring the matter to the Department of Health.

About a week after my visit with the Minister for Health at his clinic in Wexford I received a phone call from his office asking me to attend a meeting with the minister and others at the Department in Dublin. This, I thought, was the breakthrough I had been waiting for: now I could make the truth known to the highest medical authority in the land. I thought that when I told them what I knew, they would waste no more time and instigate an immediate and thorough investigation.

I asked Kate Craig for her advice on what I should say to these people. She drafted a letter for me to take along, stating that she had instigated legal proceedings against the National Maternity Hospital on my behalf and that any information I would disclose to them was privileged. She reminded me that we were now fighting the system and I should not get my hopes up too high. There was no reason to suppose that the minister would take on the might of the medical profession. So with all that in mind, I went to Dublin on a rainy Monday armed with the letter, the terrible truth and the hope that after today everything would be different and I would no longer be alone.

The Department of Health is housed in Hawkins House, a tall grey office block not far from Trinity College. I entered the reception area and explained to a man at the desk that I had an appointment with the minister. After a short wait I was met and escorted upstairs by another man. Arriving at a smaller reception area I was again asked to wait and directed to a small waiting area with chairs and a table. After another short wait I was led by the minister's secretary along a corridor to a large, brightly lit conference room. The minister was already there and was talking with the other people in the room. When they became aware of my presence their conversation stopped and the minister came over and greeted me. He then intro-

duced me to the other men in the room. They were Dr
Tim Collins (Minister's Policy Adviser), Mr Donal
Devitt (Assistant Secretary, Secondary Care Division),
and Dr Niall Tierney (Chief Medical Officer).

We all moved to a long table and sat down. I sat at
the top of one end with the minister and his secretary
sitting at the opposite end. The others sat at the sides
and produced pens from their pockets. When everyone seemed settled in their chairs I spoke. I told them
that before we started I would like them to read the
letter that my solicitor had drafted. I produced the
envelope and passed it around. When each of them
had finished reading it they passed it on to the next.
There was silence as the letter passed from hand to
hand until it reached the last man on the chain. He
said that he was not happy with the contents of the
letter and would not feel comfortable agreeing with it.
This caused a kind of pregnant silence in the room
and the man suddenly realized that everyone was
looking at him. He saw that he was the only one there
who had a problem with the letter and almost immediately changed his mind when I said that I would
leave if he wasn't happy.

When I had finished telling Gerardine's story, I

thanked them and asked them to please help me to get the truth told. I told them that I wanted to bury my wife and stop the prolonged suffering that Gerardine's family and I were going through. I told them that other women were going to die there unless they did something to make the National Maternity Hospital realize that their system was flawed. I finished off by saying that when the case eventually did come to court, I would win. 'I will win my hollow victory,' I said, 'and I will shame them all.'

The minister walked me to the lift and we shook hands. I gasped for air as I walked out the front door of Hawkins House. It was as if I had been through a battle and although I wasn't sure if I had won or lost, I felt that I had fought well, told the truth and kept my dignity. It was up to them, now. They had the power to make the hospital tell the truth. They had the power and the duty to help me. They would have to do something, if only to stop any further unnecessary deaths at the National Maternity Hospital.

THE DAYS PASSED into weeks without any reply from the Department of Health. I waited anxiously for a letter or a phone call that might help end this seemingly endless nightmare, but none came. Then, in June 1994, almost three months later, I woke to find a letter from the Minister for Health lying in the hallway. I scooped it up and ripped it open thinking that at last they had decided to do the right thing. The letter read:

Dear Constituent,

I write to you on a personal basis to seek your support for the Labour Party candidates in the European Election on Thursday, 9th June.

I believe that I have represented Wexford well since my election to Dail Eireann. I also believe that the Labour Party in Government has proven that things can be different and that people come first in Government policies.

In order to reflect this view in the European Parliament, I would respectfully ask you to give your vote on Thursday to:

> *NO. 1 SEAMUS PATTISON*
>
> *NO. 2 MICHAEL BELL*

Best wishes,

Yours sincerely,
Brendan Howlin, T.D.
Minister for Health

The Bin-Bag

I have had this letter framed, along with the bills from the hospital. They hang on the wall in my music room. I knew that if I ever felt like giving up, all I would have to do was look at them.

NINE / *The Madhouse*

L et's look back and see where I stood at that time.
Everyone in authority had turned their backs on
me. The legal case was going to take years to get to
court. The hospital was continuing with its business
as if nothing had happened. When I approached Dr
Harrison at the Rotunda in hope that he might be able
to do something, he said, and I quote: 'I can't afford to
get involved, I have to work with these people.'

I was paying periodic visits to the National Maternity Hospital, especially around the anniversary of
Gerardine's death. I would make my way through the
front door and up the stairs to Unit 4. I would walk
down the hall and turn left past the nurse's station
and into the ward. There I would stand and look for

some minutes at the bed where Gerardine was kept for those nine horrible days. I would then turn around and walk back towards the nurse's station. There I would present to those present a packet of rubbish sacks and one of Gerardine's memorial cards. To whatever doctor or nurses were there at the time I would always ask the same question: 'Did you kill anyone today?' They usually just stood there looking at their feet. My presence there made them very uncomfortable indeed. I had two reasons for paying them these visits: to remind them of their arrogance, and to try to prevent them from doing to any other woman what they did to Gerardine. When I felt that I had made my point, I would turn around and walk back down the hall, down the stairs and out into the street.

All that I was sure of was that outside those in my employ and a few family members, nobody cared. The days were turning into weeks and the weeks into years. I was turning into a bona fide, card-carrying heartless bastard. By day I found myself plotting against my enemies and by night enduring the torments of a man abandoned by all. There were times when the anger would become so intense that I would scream out loud. I would pace the floor for hours talking to myself. I would relive Gerardine's last hours and substitute myself for her. I tortured myself. I blamed myself for not guarding her. It had been my job to protect her and I had failed. I felt guilty that I was alive and Gerardine wasn't. I absolutely hated those who were responsible for her death. I had created an impenetrable and wretched world for myself and I excluded all others from it.

NOW, I SAT and waited for the doctor to finish his surgery. This was a doctor that I had no argument with. We had grown up together and gone to the same school. I had come to a point where I had to risk reaching out to someone in the hope that I could be rescued from myself. This was not easy for me. I wanted to feel that all doctors were bad. Reaching out to a member of what I considered to be the enemy might well have been the cry for help that so often gets missed. There is no place for rational thought when you are so emotionally charged and driven by such a potent force as pure hatred. It was probably instinct that brought me there that evening. I needed a way out.

My doctor friend walked out of his surgery and made his way towards me, sitting on the step beside me. He didn't speak. He just sat there looking out across the street and waited. He had been very close to what had happened. He was our doctor and I knew that Gerardine's death had affected him deeply. He knew that I was there to talk and he waited until I was ready.

I lit a cigarette and proceeded to tell him everything. It was a strange open-air confessional. I told it all with hardly a pause for breath. It felt like I was trying to drag the monkey from my back and it didn't want to go. I spoke in an even monotone, but the words themselves were screaming. The power and the content of what I told him evidently shocked him. He quickly realized the extent of my torment and when he spoke he did so in a very measured and focused way. He asked me if I would consider 'seeing someone'. He said that if I would let him, he would help me. He said that he would arrange for me to see a psychiatrist. I smiled and told him that I didn't have much faith in psychiatry. He smiled back and assured me that some psychiatrists can, in fact, help us. 'Theirs is probably the toughest job of all,' he said. I thanked him for listening and left saying that I would think about it. Later that evening he rang and told me that he had arranged for me to see a lady psychiatrist the next morning at St Dymphna's mental hospital in Carlow. He said that for everyone's sake, I should really consider going. I told him that I would and I could almost hear a sigh of relief coming down the phone line. My decision to talk to him had been a good one. He was and is a good doctor, but more importantly he is a good human being and at that time I needed to discover a good human being, particularly in the medical profession.

FOR THE FIRST TIME in my life I walked through the doors of a mental hospital. I had walked across the grounds of this hospital a million times as a youngster, on the way down to the river to swim and have adventures. We would sometimes peek through the hedges at the back of the hospital and the patients inside. I remember how lifeless and forlorn the inmates looked. They shuffled along, their eyes staring and glazed over, their speech garbled and incoherent. We were too young to understand that they were for the most part drugged into complete passivity. They could no longer lock people up for just being mad, so they pacified them with tranquillizers and herded them around like helpless wandering sheep. The care and treatment of these forgotten human beings was never seen as a major priority. So many of them were just dumped into these institutions by their families. A lot of them were just old and unwanted, or alcoholics placed there because no one knew what to do with them. I remember as a very young child being frightened at the huge grey walls that surrounded the place. I also remember when I was in primary school, watching them take the walls down and allowing the public to walk freely through the beautiful gardens.

As I walked inside this familiar brown-grey building, I saw how old and Victorian it looked. It had the usual look of an Irish institution bequeathed by the retreating British. Inside were long corridors with marbled floors and gloss-painted walls and ceilings. The only apparent difference that I could see between this and the likes of the National Maternity Hospital was that here there was no sickly smell of antiseptic. I found the reception and was told there that I was expected and the doctor would see me shortly. I remember entering the psychiatrist's office and immediately looking around the room for the couch. There wasn't one. It looked just like any doctor's office with the exception of the pictures of body parts and eye charts.

Dr Horgan welcomed me in and I sat down facing her. She started by saying that she had been talking to my doctor friend, who had asked her to see me. She admitted that she knew little of what had happened to Gerardine, but from what my doctor had told her she understood that I was having some problems. She asked me to tell her in detail what had happened to Gerardine and what was happening to me. I took a deep breath and recounted the whole nightmare. I noticed the same growing look of alarm that I had seen on the face of my doctor friend, as the psychiatrist began to realize the full extent of what I was telling her. She asked me one or two questions here and there, but overall I think she knew that this was far beyond what she was used to dealing with. She tried not to show it, but she was obviously very affected by what I had told her, and when I had finished talking there was an awkward silence in the room. I broke the silence by thanking her for listening, saying that I had to be elsewhere. I'm sure that she wanted to try to help me, and she asked me one or two more fairly standard questions, but I had obviously caught her off guard. This story was bigger than both of us.

LATER THAT EVENING I received a phone call from my doctor friend saying that he had just finished talking to with Dr Horgan and that she was extremely concerned about my condition. She had said she knew of only one psychiatrist in this country who could understand this kind of anger and she had taken it upon herself to contact him in the hope that he would agree to see me. He said that he would, and now my doctor friend was asking me if I would agree to go see him. I told him I would and he gave me the details. I now had an appointment at the Central Mental Hospital in Dundrum, Dublin. The man I was going to see was Dr Charles Smith, the medical director of the institution. I had heard this place mentioned occasionally on the news as the destination of the criminally insane. I didn't have any idea what to expect when I got there. I did think that there was a chance that they might not let me back out. Whatever my fears might have been, I had given my word that I would go.

The first thing I saw was the high grey wall, broken in the middle by the main entrance. I stopped my car in front of a high steel gate that guarded this entrance and waited. Inside and to the left, I could see a small gate-lodge out of which two men came to open the gate. I drove up a little and gave my name and stated my business. I was expected and was given instructions where to go. The main gate opened into a small kind of holding area that was surrounded by a high steel fence. At the opposite end of the fence was another steel gate that would lead inside to the hospital itself. This gate was controlled electronically and opened as if by magic as I drove towards it. I was greeted by neat buildings surrounded by well-kept gardens. I was heading for what the gate man called the 'new building' and I found it without any difficulty. Again I found myself in a reception area waiting.

After some minutes, I noticed a man at the edge of the reception area and looked up. 'Mr Gleeson?' he asked. 'Hello,' I replied and rose from my seat to shake his hand. He looked at me for some time, perhaps trying to reconcile the information that he had received about me with the man now standing in front of him. He led me to his office and offered me a chair. He sat opposite me, still looking intently at me. He spoke first, saying that if he felt that I was going to be a danger to anyone he was duty-bound to inform them and this was something that I should know from the start. I replied that I had no problem with that and said that we all have to do what we think is right.

He asked me to tell him the full story and I did. He listened intently, stopping me in places to ask a question or clear up a point he didn't understand. I told him every detail that I could remember and at times I broke down in tears, particularly when I was explaining Gerardine's last days in the custody of the National Maternity Hospital. I think it took about an hour to tell the entire story and in all that time his interest never waned. He was very patient with me, especially when I broke down in tears. I was so emotionally charged that when I did become upset, I would hyperventilate and had to stop talking and try to catch my breath.

At the beginning his questions were of a general nature. He asked me about myself, my childhood and my relationship with Gerardine. As the story progressed his questions became more probing. I began to feel that he was asking me all the right questions and he was asking them in the right way. He was building for himself a picture of who I was and I liked the way that he was doing it. When I had finished telling my story, I think that we both looked very different to each other. He now knew something of me and I felt that this was a man I could talk to.

For the next three years I would visit him once a week, and then once a fortnight for two years more. He never judged me. He told me that I had every right to feel the way I did. He very skilfully took my life apart and made me look closely at it. He told me from the beginning that this was going to take a long time and it wasn't going to be easy on either of us. He said that he was going to try to find out where my anger really began and in the end I think he probably did. At the end of my first visit with him, he said that he would help me, but on one condition. He asked me to promise him that I wouldn't hurt anyone. I told him that I didn't think I could make that promise. There was an awkward moment and I thought that I had closed a window of opportunity. He then gave us both a way out, saying that if I did feel that I was going to hurt someone, I must promise to speak to him first. He was perceptive enough even after meeting me only once to know that I wouldn't break a promise.

TEN / *A Good Day*

As Charlie Smith was busy trying to put my anger in perspective, Kate Craig was busy putting our legal case together. On my now frequent visits with her, I noticed how the files were getting fatter. It was now five years since Gerardine's death. When we began, the file consisted of three lonely pages in a brown folder. Now there were numerous bound stacks of documents piled on a table in front of us. They consisted of medical reports, statements, letters, and affidavits. There were hundreds of hand-written notes in the margins of the pages, and it was clear that she had meticulously examined every one. The amount of work that she was doing was incredible. My confidence in her and her ability was total. Kate was at all times sympathetic to my feelings and the feelings of Gerardine's family. She knew only too well the full horror of Gerardine's death and how it had affected us all. She showed great patience and understanding when interviewing both Gerardine's family and myself. She never let emotion cloud the facts. She was always aware that we were up against a very powerful and resourceful system. That system and the people involved in defending it would do everything in their power to find the smallest fault in our case. Kate wasn't going to give them any loophole to crawl out of. We could only assume that they too were going over this case with a fine-toothed comb looking for a way out. I knew that Kate was never going to give them that chance.

Apart from the report that we had received from Professor Bonnar, we commissioned a second medical report from Professor R.W. Shaw, head of the department of obstetrics and gynaecology at the University of Wales College of Medicine. His report was similarly damning. Like Professor Bonnar, Professor Shaw stated that Gerardine's bowel obstruction should have been apparent almost immediately after her admission to the National Maternity Hospital. He said further that at the time of her final illness Gerardine showed no signs of ovarian hyperstimulation syndrome, which was what she was being treated for. He concluded by noting that Gerardine's case 'illustrates how easily once a wrong diagnosis is made other problems are ignored to the detriment of the patient'.

I WAS DOING the occasional gig with the Linda Martin band. Linda, a former Eurovision Song Contest winner, would occasionally ask me to play guitar with her when she was working in Ireland. Playing music was my only distraction from Gerardine's death. The two hours or so spent on a stage concentrating on the music seemed to be the only respite I could find. Some months prior to our first visit to the High Court, Linda rang me to ask if I was available to do a gig one Friday night in the Burlington Hotel in Dublin. I said yes and arrived on the appointed night for the sound check. As was often the case, neither I nor the other occasional members of Linda's band had any idea of whom or what the gig was for.

When we had finished the sound check, we all gathered in the hotel lobby and waited for the punters to arrive and have their meal. When they had finished eating and making whatever speeches had to be made, it was our turn to provide them with the music to dance to for the rest of the evening. We sat at a table and had our tea and watched as the punters arrived, the men in dinner jackets and dicky bows and the women in ball gowns. I remember saying that this looked like a very posh affair indeed. Then Linda mentioned that it was the Royal College of Surgeons Ball. This didn't make any impression on me at the time.

Eventually we changed into our black attire and took the stage. Soon everyone was out dancing and having a good time. About a half hour into the show, Linda announced that there was a special request from the audience: 'Could we have Professor Robert Harrison up here to sing a song?' I couldn't believe my ears. Then I saw him emerge from the crowd. He made his way up to the stage. He took the microphone from Linda and then walked over to me and said he was going to do some rock and roll. I was sure that at any second he was going to realize who he was talking to. For a moment I thought that he did, but he just turned towards the front of the stage and started singing 'Johnny B. Goode'. We all fell in behind him as he proceeded to murder the Chuck Berry classic. When the time came I played my twelve-bar solo while he reeled around the stage like a rock star. I couldn't believe it: here was a man I loathed, on stage with me, and I was making him sound good.

When the song was finished he made his way up to me and announced his next intended victim. By now he was really getting into it, and some of the younger members of the audience were standing at the front of the stage and cheering him on. Again there were solos to be played, and I played them while he assumed the role of rock and roll hero. Finally he left the stage with the sound of applause in his ears.

I was stunned: I couldn't believe that after everything that had happened he didn't recognize me. It was clear that I had made no impression on him at all on that day in his office at the Rotunda when I had asked him if he could help. The rest of the gig went more or less as usual and I watched as he took the floor and danced with his wife. When the gig was over I stepped off the stage and made my way over to where the professor was sitting. When he saw me coming he shot up from his seat in a welcoming manner; I suppose he thought I was going to congratulate him on his performance. He opened his mouth to speak but before he got the words out I said, 'Do you not recognize me?' He looked a little puzzled and turned towards his wife, then said that he didn't. I asked him if the 4th of August 1993 meant anything to him and he replied, 'No, it doesn't.' I saw that his wife sensed that all was not as it seemed with the questions I was asking her husband, but he was on a high and even put his arm around me. 'The 4th of August 1993,' he repeated to himself. Then he asked, 'Did your wife have a baby on that day?' I leaned towards him and whispered into his ear, 'That's the day my beautiful wife died, you fuck.' He stood there for a few seconds transfixed. Then the penny dropped, and he blurted, 'Oh, I'm sorry.' 'Sorry is not good enough,' I said, and walked away through the crowd.

I WAS STILL regularly visiting Charlie Smith at the Central Mental Hospital. The anger was still there and as large as life, but he was helping me to control it. He made the point of telling me that I was not insane. My anger was extreme, but completely natural. He was slowly helping me to understand myself. I have never lost my hatred and I hope I never will. This was one concession that he allowed me. He said that if I found it in my heart to forgive them, even when they didn't deserve it, then I would almost surely overcome the anger. This concept, although noble, was a non-runner. I was used to hating them now. It was the only thing that kept me going.

I STOOD on the quays with my back to the river and looked closely at the building in front of me. The Four Courts, another imperial construction. In less than two weeks' time I would be going inside for my day in the High Court. I was in Dublin that day to meet my barrister for the second time. Kate Craig had secured the services of Liam Reidy, Senior Counsel. It was now time for a final council of war. Liam's office was not far from the Four Courts building itself, in a fairly modern building down a narrow cobbled lane near Smithfield market. I had arrived early for my appointment and used the time to take in my surroundings. Kate had asked Charlie Smith to come to this meeting, and as luck would have it we came across each other on the street leading to my barrister's office. As we made our way in to the courtyard in front of the office building we met Kate and we all went inside together. It was a nice, relaxed atmosphere. We made small talk. We sat around a table and had some tea. Kate and Liam sat at one side of the table and Charlie and myself at the other.

What happened next took me completely by surprise. Liam said that because of the meticulous work Kate had done in putting the case together, the hospital had admitted negligence. He said it in an even and relaxed tone that at first made me think that he was making some kind of joke. How could this be true? I looked over at Charlie and I could see that he too was at a loss for a response. It must have taken me several minutes to grasp what he had said. When my head had cleared a little I finally asked, 'You mean they just gave up?' He said that that was exactly what had happened, but that the news wasn't all good. I had to pause then and ask him what he meant by that. He said that they had admitted liability on behalf of the 'junior' staff only. He then said that I should take some time and gather my thoughts and that there were some important decisions that I had to make.

I excused myself and went outside to have a ciga-

rette. The game had changed completely. On the one
hand the hospital had finally admitted its liability, but
on the other hand they were blaming the junior staff
and in that way making it sound like a mistake made
by junior personnel and thus somehow almost acceptable. I knew that Liam was trying not to put pressure
on me to make any decision that I felt I couldn't live
with. After some time I returned to Liam's office and
said that the hospital's admission of liability on behalf
of the junior staff was unacceptable.

WE SPENT the rest of that afternoon going over our
case. There were some minor details to be cleared up
and Liam explained to me how our case was going to
be presented. The case that we were bringing against
them was not just for the negligence that brought
about Gerardine's death, but also for the psychologi-
cal damage that they had inflicted upon me. The damage to me and the manner in which the hospital
behaved towards Gerardine's family and myself was a
part of the case that I insisted upon. It was never going
to be enough for me to just let them admit that their
negligence had led to Gerardine's death. There is lim-

ited compensation payable when negligence causes a death and this would be easily payable by the hospital's insurance company. I was never going to let them get away that easily. By insisting on including myself in the case against them, they would now be faced with the possibility of paying very substantial damages. Liam explained that when we did go to the High Court they might make a monetary offer and asked me if I was prepared to listen to any offer that might be made. I told him that I would do a deal with them if they publicly admitted their liability, unreservedly and without the word 'junior' involved, and also apologized publicly. He smiled when I said this and replied, 'You're not looking for much, are you?'

GERARDINE'S SISTER Noelline had agreed to come to the High Court with me. I was glad that she was coming; it was only right that someone from Gerardine's family should be there. I collected her at 5.30 a.m. on Wednesday the 10th of July 1998. We went to the cemetery and said a prayer at Gerardine's grave. I asked Gerardine for the strength to keep myself together and remain strong. I picked up a small white stone from her grave and put it in my pocket. We then began our journey towards Dublin and the High Court.

We arrived around seven and waited for Kate Craig to arrive. We had arranged to meet her in what is known as the Round Hall, a reception area where people congregate before they begin their cases or draw their judges. We had arrived a bit early and were the only ones there. There were notice-boards dotted around the room with lists of cases on them and we inspected them looking for ours. I looked down the list and eventually came upon: 'JOHN GLEESON-V-THE NATIONAL MATERNITY HOSPITAL'. My heart jumped a little. The atmosphere of the place was very intimidating. I could feel a tremendous sense of apprehension. We were not the only people coming here looking for justice and I could easily pick out the faces of other plaintiffs whose body language betrayed their nervousness.

Kate arrived and we went and had some tea. I had to force myself to eat something. I hadn't slept the night before and I had smoked about a million ciga-rettes. I knew that it would be important for me to eat something, so I had some bread and tea. I was so tense that I couldn't even taste what I was eating and I just went through the mechanics of feeding myself. Kate had arranged a room for us downstairs. This would be our base. We were allowing for the case to take about ten days so it was going to be important for us to have somewhere to talk privately and make decisions. After we had something to eat we went down to this room and waited for Liam to arrive. Kate, as always, was great. She knew the case inside-out. She exuded confidence and I drew a lot of strength from her.

Liam arrived and greeted us warmly. He told us what court we were in and what judge we had drawn. He asked me again if I had considered doing a deal with them. I replied that I would if they admitted everything and apologized. He said that he under-stood and then excused himself, saying that he would see us upstairs in the courtroom.

As we made our way up I remember feeling almost like a condemned man being led to the gal-lows. We passed a group of people who were in seri-ous and intense conversation with their barrister. There was a girl in the midst of this group crying her eyes out and an older woman, probably her mother, trying to comfort her. The emotion of it all was just too much for this girl to take. I knew how she felt. I reached into my pocket and retrieved the small white stone that I had earlier removed from Gerardine's grave. I put it in my left hand and held it firmly. I said a silent prayer to Gerardine and told her that if she minded me today, I wouldn't let go of this stone until I was able to put it back on her grave where it belonged.

When we arrived at the courtroom there were already a lot of people inside. I went in and sat on a seat to the left of the door, facing across the room. From where I was sitting I could see everyone in the room and they could see me. At the head of the court-room was a kind of enclosed desk on a low platform where the judge would sit. Attached to this was the witness box. In front of this platform was a long table behind which sat the court stenographer and all the solicitors including Kate. They sat facing outwards towards the back of the room. In front of the solicitors was a series of long benches. The National Maternity Hospital defence team occupied the right-hand side of the first bench. Liam sat on the left side. Behind them on the next bench sat their junior counsel. Behind Liam there was one man; behind Mary Irvine, senior counsel for the National Maternity Hospital, there was a whole team of junior counsel.

Liam began to read from the book of pleadings. He told the story of Gerardine's death. He explained that the case being brought against the National Maternity Hospital was for 'nervous shock'. This was a result of the trauma that I had suffered because of the circumstances of Gerardine's death and the horrific manner in which she died. It's worth mentioning that in all these proceedings I never saw one doctor or nurse from the hospital in court. They never had the decency to face their accuser.

When Liam had finished outlining the case against the hospital he thanked the judge and sat down. It was then the turn of Mary Irvine to respond. She admitted liability for the hospital on behalf of its junior staff, but she argued that the case for damages arising from 'nervous shock' suffered by me was a different one from what they understood from the book of pleadings. For some time arguments were put forth on both sides as to the nature of the case being brought. In the end it was decided to adjourn the case for mention and the defence asked for all my medical records to be supplied to them for examination. It was also agreed that I would be assessed by a psychiatrist of the defence's choosing.

WE RETURNED HOME in the early evening and I replaced the stone on Gerardine's grave. I sat in my usual spot by the grave and reflected on what had happened that day. It reminded me of David and Goliath. On the one side there was the hospital's huge defence team with all its expertise, power and resources, and on the other side was Liam and his junior counsel. But it only looked one-sided. The power of our argument swelled our number a hundredfold. When Liam stood up in the court and read out the details of Gerardine's death I could see the effect it was having. The tragic truth was on our side and everyone there knew it. The hospital's defence team had just bought themselves some time and all we had to do now was wait.

It was some weeks later before the hospital's defence team arranged for a psychiatrist for me to see. When I received the details from my solicitor, I asked Charlie if he knew of this psychiatrist. Charlie said that he did and that the man had good reputation and would give an honest and fair account in his assessment of me. This was encouraging. My one fear was that I would be going to visit someone who had been instructed by some insurance company not to assess me but to undermine me. I knew in my heart that if this man was willing to listen with an open mind then this was a straw that the hospital's defence team would be wasting their time clutching at.

I went to visit the psychiatrist and he proved to be just as professional as Charlie had said. I spent quite some time with him and when I left I was in no doubt that he too was affected by the tragedy of Gerardine's death and the effect it had on me. I felt that he would tell the truth and that his assessment of me would strengthen our case beyond anything the hospital could defend.

I COLLECTED NOELLINE at 5.30 on Wednesday morning the 28th of October 1998, and we went directly to the cemetery. Again we said a short prayer and again I took a small white stone from the grave and put it in my pocket. In my prayer I asked Gerardine to watch over us and I asked God to watch over

Gerardine's soul. We then headed off into the bright-
ening morning towards Dublin and the High Court. It
felt right. I had the feeling that our time had finally
come. This time there were no feelings of apprehension when we entered the Four Courts and waited for
Kate and Liam to meet us. We sat in the Round Hall
and took in the now-familiar sight. Kate arrived first
and told us that everything was ready for the case
ahead. This time they would have to address the case
we were presenting them with. Liam arrived shortly
after and introduced me to another senior counsel
whom he had asked to join our team. We were not so
small now. There was an air of quiet confidence
amongst them all. I knew that they had all taken this
case to their hearts. They all approached this case in a
professional manner at all times, but I knew from the
way they acted that the tragedy of Gerardine's death
had touched them on a personal level too. They had
examined every minute detail surrounding Gerardine's death and they wouldn't be human if it hadn't
touched them in some way.

We drew our judge and court number and made
our way to it. As we approached the courtroom I saw
that we were going to win. The defence team had

shrunk beyond all recognition. Mary Irvine was still there, but instead of the large team of black-robed barristers who had been in attendance at the last hearing, this time she had just two assistants with her.

While we waited in the hallway to go inside I noticed that Liam was engaged in serious conversation with Mary Irvine. After some minutes he broke away and approached me. He asked me if I remembered telling him what my conditions were if they offered any kind of deal. I told him that I did and that it wasn't negotiable. He smiled at me and said, 'They have offered to apologize.'

'Publicly?' I asked

'Yes,' he said.

I then asked him if they were going to admit liability on behalf of the entire hospital and not the junior staff. He then produced a piece of paper and asked me to write down what it was I wanted them to say. I wrote that I wanted them to admit negligence in the diagnosis and treatment of Gerardine. I wanted them also to apologize to me and to Gerardine's family for all the grief that they had caused. When I had finished writing Liam took the piece of paper, looked at it and smiled. He then went down the hall to the hospital's senior counsel and presented her with it. She made a series of calls on her mobile phone. We sat and waited patiently. After some of these calls she would again engage in serious conversation with Liam. After one such discussion Liam approached me and said that the hospital would agree to apologize, but only on behalf of the junior staff. I instantly replied 'No deal' and he returned to Mary Irvine with that message. The phone calls continued and after some time Liam told me that they were trying to convene a special meeting of the board of directors of the hospital. He said that they couldn't locate one of their members and that was causing something of a delay. This whole thing was beginning to drag and the judge was showing remarkable patience.

From time to time Liam would return with the latest proposal from the hospital regarding changes that they wanted made to the wording of the apology. My answer was always the same. Liam knew that I wouldn't change my mind; he was just keeping me posted. It would have been interesting to be a fly on the wall at Holles Street that morning as the hospital received updates from the Four Courts and weighed the pros and cons of making the apology that I was asking for. If they made the apology, they might be able to limit the damages paid by them for their negligence in the care of Gerardine's. If they did not, they risked being forced to pay a potentially very large award arising from the nervous shock I had suffered as a result of the ordeal.

So as the battle raged elsewhere we continued to sit and wait. The phone calls continued and before long it was lunchtime. Noelline, Kate and I went downstairs and across the road to a pub to have our lunch. We didn't discuss the case. I wasn't sure whether they would agree to the terms I had specified. I knew if we pursued the case as it was now being presented against them in the book of pleadings, we would win and the damages that they would have to pay would be very large indeed. Their only real option was to surrender and finally tell the truth.

WE RETURNED after lunch and on my way back up the stairs I took the small white stone from my pocket and held it in my left hand. We resumed our wait in the hallway outside the courtroom. At that time there were just the three of us sitting on a bench under one of the windows. I remember seeing Liam enter through a door at the far end of the hall and walking towards us. His face betrayed no emotion. When he reached us he stopped beside me and put his hand on my shoulder. 'Congratulations,' he said. 'You won. They have agreed to make the statement exactly as you have worded it.' He was smiling now and said, 'This is more than a victory. This is something unheard of. These people never publicly apologize. This is the first time that I have ever heard of it happening.'

I turned towards Noelline and I could see tears in her eyes. We both stood up and she put her arms around me. 'You did it,' she whispered in my ear, 'you beat them'.

'*We* beat them,' I said. 'We beat them with the truth.' I turned toward Liam and shook his hand and thanked him. I then went over to Kate. I told her that I just didn't have the words. She smiled at me and simply said, 'You're welcome.'

We then went into the courtroom. Of all the strange feelings I have had in the years since Gerardine's death, the feeling that I experienced now was as strange as any. I was not elated. I didn't feel any sense of victory, whatever that is. I wasn't suddenly transformed into a happy man. I don't really remember feeling anything at all. I think that I had been filled with such a passionate hatred for so many years that I wasn't capable of allowing any other emotion to touch me.

What was I going to do now? Bringing the hospital to justice was the only life I knew. I hadn't considered what the future might hold. If I felt anything at all it was a feeling of sorrow. I didn't want it to be over. I needed this whole thing to keep me alive. For the first time since I was a child I felt afraid. Hating those who allowed Gerardine to die was the crutch that I leaned on, but now I realized that I wouldn't have that excuse any more. I'd have to face her death all over again, this time as a grieving husband and not as a vengeful one.

We all stood up and the judge took his place behind his bench. When everyone had settled he asked us to begin and Liam stood up and explained to the judge that an agreement had been reached between both parties. Liam went on to say that as part of this agreement a statement was to be made to the court by the senior counsel representing the National Maternity Hospital. Then Mary Irvine rose from her seat and addressed the court. She said that the hospi-

135

tal acknowledged its negligence in the diagnosis and treatment of Mrs Gerardine Gleeson and they wished to apologize to Mr John Gleeson and his late wife's family for the distress that this caused. She then thanked the court and sat down. Noelline then had to go into the witness box and make a short statement on behalf of Gerardine's family.

When Noelline had finished the judge thanked everyone present and said that he hoped that this would bring to a conclusion this sad and tragic case. He then turned towards me and offered his sympathies on the tragic death of my wife. I thanked him and he then closed the proceedings. We all stood up as the judge left. When we sat down again Mary Irvine and one her assistants came over and shook my hand. The assistant said that she was sorry for my troubles. I respected that. I held no grudge against the hospital's lawyers. It was a very human gesture that the barrister's assistant made and I took it as such. The other woman that was part of their team stayed in her seat. She didn't look like she was having a good day.

THERE WAS a reporter from *The Irish Times* waiting in

the hall and he asked me one or two questions. He told me that there were photographers waiting to take my picture outside the front door of the courthouse. I was beginning to realize the enormity of what we had achieved. It had taken five years, one month, twenty-four days and two hours to do it. All I had ever wanted was for the hospital to tell me the truth. That's all I had asked the Master of the hospital, Peter Boylan, to tell me. That's what I had asked the Minister for Health, Brendan Howlin, to get for me. Of all the doctors and nurses from the National Maternity Hospital, in whose care Gerardine was supposed to have been, not one of them ever even had the decency to say to me that they were sorry, even if it was just that they were sorry that Gerardine had died. The apology that they made to me and to Gerardine's family in court would always be just a symbol. If they were really sorry for what they did then none of this would have been necessary. Allowing Gerardine to die in that medieval manner was a mistake on their part, but everything that they did after that was planned. They adopted a siege mentality and closed ranks when threatened. They personify the arrogance of those in a position of power. This arrogance flowed from the most senior staff right down to the most junior. The bills and the bin-bag were just symptoms of their contempt for the common person. Gerardine was never a person to them. She was just another public patient in their way.

I SAID GOODBYE to my small but stalwart legal team and thanked them again from the bottom of my heart. As we left the courthouse a group of photographers began to take pictures of me. We then walked around towards Smithfield market where my car was parked and began on our journey home. When we reached Carlow, I dropped Noelline off at her house and made my way to the cemetery. I knelt beside Gerardine's grave, opened my left hand, and placed the small white stone back where it belonged. This grave was the place where I had made my promise to her that I was going to bring them to justice. I knelt there for a long time. I began to feel a kind of peace. It had been a long time since I had felt this way. It was as if when I released the small white stone from my hand that I was beginning to remove the monkey from my back. I remember suddenly becoming very weak and

I had to hold on to the headstone for balance. I was overcome by emotion and I wept like a child.

Later that night as I sat watching the 9 o'clock news, I heard the newsreader report that the National Maternity Hospital had made an apology to the husband and family of a Carlow woman, Mrs Gerardine Gleeson. The newsreader went on to say that the hospital had also admitted negligence in the diagnosis and treatment of Mrs Gleeson.

I slept well enough that night and was awoken the next morning by a knocking on my front door. I opened the door to a local taxi driver with a piece of paper in his hand. He said that I was to ring this number, and handed me the paper. The number was for Pat Kenny's radio show; my telephone number is ex-directory, and the researchers had obviously gone to great lengths to contact me. I rang the number and was immediately interviewed by Pat Kenny. He asked me about the apology and how long I had been waiting for it. He asked about Gerardine's death and I recounted the whole story for him. He made me feel very comfortable and showed great sympathy and understanding. When the interview was finished he thanked me and conveyed his condolences on the death of my wife. I then dressed quickly and sat by the radio to listen to the interview, which had been recorded. The reaction began immediately. People from all over the country began to ring in to the show to offer their condolences to me and to Gerardine's family. I learned later that literally hundreds of people called the show to offer their sympathy. Some of these callers were interviewed later in the show; one woman talked about her own experience with a hospital and its fondness for bin-bags.

The minute the radio show finished my telephone began to ring. At first it was calls from people I knew. Then I started receiving calls from strangers who just wanted to say how sorry they were to hear what had happened to Gerardine. The phone never stopped all day. I'll never know how these people got my telephone number. For about four days newspaper reporters called to the house. Every day on his show Pat Kenny would read out more reactions from people who had phoned in about Gerardine's death. I was touched by this response from so many strangers, who shared some of my sadness and outrage at what had been done to my beautiful wife Gerardine. I knew then that I was no longer alone.

A Good Day

*

I DIDN'T DIE of a broken heart but I know that I will die with one. Gerardine and I would have grown old together. We would have collected our pensions together. Young couples would have looked at us and asked themselves if they too would be like us when they were our age. I miss my beautiful Gerardine. I miss our life.